MW00446225

Part of a Comprehensive and Systematic Program of Islamic Studies

An Enrichment Book
in the Program of Islamic History
Elementary Level

Copyright © June, 1997
IQRA' International Educational Foundation.
All Rights Reserved.

Third Printing February 2006
Printed in China

Special note on copyright:
This book is a part of IQRA's comprehensive
and systematic program of Islamic Studies
being developed for the planned Islamic
Education of Muslim children and youth.

No part of this book may be reproduced by
any means including photocopying, electronic,
mechanical, recording, or otherwise without the
written permission of the publisher. In specific
cases permission is granted on written request
to publish or translate IQRA's works.
For information regarding permission, write to:
IQRA' International Educational Foundation
7450 Skokie Blvd., Skokie, IL 60077

Library of Congress Catalog Card Number 95-82409
ISBN # 1-56316-378-0

Chief Program Editors
Dr.Abidullah al-Ansari Ghazi
(Ph.D. Harvard University)

Dr.Tasneema Ghazi
(Ph.D. University of Minnesota)

Language Editor
Mahlaqa Patel
(University of Illinois, Chicago)

Huda Quraishi
(University of Illinois, Chicago)

Typesetting:
Sabeehuddin Khaja

Design
Kathryn Heimberger
(American Academy of Art)

The Prophets of Allah

Volume III
Elementary Level

Mildred El-Amin
Suhaib Hamid Ghazi

Illustrated by Ash-har Quraishi

IQRA' International Educational Foundation

IQRA'S NOTE

We, at IQRA' International Educational Foundation, are grateful to Allāh ﷻ for enabling us to present the third volume of <u>The Prophets of Allāh</u> for our young readers. The present volume contains the life and teachings of four prophets of Allāh ﷻ (Prophet Yūsuf, Prophet Shu'aib, Prophet Mūsa, and Prophet Hārūn) as mentioned in the Qur'ān and the *Ḥadīth*.

These books are part of IQRA's comprehensive and systematic program of Islamic education. We wish to introduce our young children to the enriched field of Islamic Social Studies through the stories and teachings of the Prophets of Allāh ﷻ. This is the beginning of a comprehensive study and understanding of the role of human beings as the *Khulafā'* of Allāh ﷻ on this planet.

The stories in this volume are incorporated into IQRA's curriculum of Islamic history (Social Studies) at third grade level. It is recommended that teachers consult and study the curriculum guide for daily lesson planning and teachings. However, the stories are independent enough to be read to young non-readers in informal settings. Second to fourth graders will enjoy reading these books on their own as the readability level of these stories ranges between second and third grades.

We urge all concerned Muslims and Islamic organizations to cooperate with IQRA' and become an *'ANṢĀR* of its educational program. We believe that together we can do it, *'In shā' Allāh*.

CONTENTS

Prophet Yūsuf عليه السلام

Prophet Ibrāhīm ﷺ had two sons who were also prophets. The first was Prophet Ismā'īl ﷺ, and the younger was Prophet Isḥāq ﷺ Many of Isḥāq's children were prophets as well, including Prophet Ya'qūb ﷺ. Prophet Ya'qūb ﷺ, the grandson of Prophet Ibrāhīm ﷺ, had twelve sons. One of the youngest was Prophet Yūsuf ﷺ. Thus, Prophet Yūsuf ﷺ was clearly the product of a historic and blessed family.

Yūsuf ﷺ and his brother Bin Yāmīn were the youngest sons of Prophet Ya'qūb ﷺ. Their mother was a beautiful and intelligent woman named Rāhid. Ya'qūb's other sons had a different mother. It was clear to everyone that Prophet Ya'qūb ﷺ loved Yūsuf ﷺ very much, even more than his other children, and this made Yūsuf's half-brothers very jealous.

THE STRANGE DREAM

One night, when Yūsuf ﷺ was a young child, he had the strangest dream. In his dream, he saw eleven stars, the sun and the moon all bowing down before him! He did not know what the vision meant, but he knew that it had some significance, so the next day he rushed to his father and told him all about it.

"Oh, Father!" he exclaimed. "In my dream, I saw eleven stars and the sun and the moon all bowing down before me!"[1]

Allah ﷻ had blessed Prophet Ya'qūb ﷺ with the gift of interpreting dreams. He knew right away what his son's dream signified.

"This is a special dream from Allāh ﷻ that will one day come true," he told his child.

"The eleven stars that you saw are your eleven brothers, and the sun and the moon represent your father and mother."

Although this was indeed a blessed dream and a reason to be joyful, Ya'qūb ﷺ warned his son to be careful. "Do not tell your brothers about this dream. They will become jealous and try to hurt you."

"Allah ﷻ will teach you the meaning of dreams," he continued. "Our family will be blessed because of you, just like your grandfather, Prophet Isḥāq ﷺ and your great-grandfather, Prophet Ibrāhīm ﷺ were blessed before you."[2]

Although he was still quite young, Yūsuf ﷺ understood that Allah ﷻ had a special plan for him.

THE BROTHERS' PLAN

Yūsuf ﷺ grew to be an extremely handsome and intelligent young lad. It was clear to his brothers that he had a very special relationship with their father, and this made them very jealous. "Even though we are good sons, our father loves Yūsuf and Bin Yāmīn more than he loves us,"[3] they complained to each other.

Prophet Ya'qūb ﷺ knew that his other sons were jealous of Yūsuf ﷺ, and this bothered the elderly Prophet ﷺ. He tried to protect Yūsuf ﷺ by keeping him nearby as much as possible. He rarely left Yūsuf ﷺ alone with his other sons, fearing that they would try to hurt him.

One day, one of the brothers came up with a plan. "Why don't we kill Yūsuf or send him away to a far off land?" he asked his brothers. "Then, we won't have to share our father's love with him."

The other brothers felt that it was much too cruel to kill their own brother, so they discussed other possibilities.

"I have a better idea," suggested another. "Why don't we throw him into the well and leave him there? Some travellers are sure to find him when they stop to fetch water!"[4] The other brothers liked this idea very much. They could quickly get rid of Yūsuf ﷺ without having to kill him. They spent many hours detailing their devious plan.

The next morning, the brothers went to their father. "O Father," they said innocently. "Will you please let Yūsuf come play with us today? We will take good care of him."[5]

But Prophet Ya'qūb ﷺ did not trust his sons. He tried to find reasons for not allowing Yūsuf ﷺ to go with them.

"What if a wolf comes and takes him away while you are not looking?"[6] he asked.

"We are a large group, and we are strong enough to fight off any wolves that may try to harm our brother,"[7] they quickly replied. Prophet Ya'qūb ﷺ sighed. Although he still felt uneasy, he gave in and allowed Yūsuf ﷺ to go with them.

Yūsuf ﷺ followed his brothers to the distant field where they had planned their scheme, not knowing what was about to happen to him. As they approached the well, the brothers looked around to make sure that they were not being watched. Suddenly, they grabbed young Yūsuf ﷺ as his back was turned. They stripped his shirt off and tossed him into the well, where he landed with a splash.

Yūsuf ﷺ could not believe what was happening! He had always known that his brothers were not very loving towards him, but this was something he had never expected.

Ignoring Yūsuf's cries for help, his brothers held a quick meeting to discuss their next move. According to the plan, they slaughtered a nearby goat and soaked Yūsuf's tattered shirt in its blood.

When they finally reached home, it was getting dark. Before they entered the house, they purposely made tears fall from their eyes. Then together, they ran into the house screaming and crying.

"Oh Father!" they pretended to weep. "Something horrible has happened to Yūsuf! We left him to watch our things while we raced. When we returned, he was gone! We think that he was taken by a wolf!"[8] The boys showed him the bloody shirt.

Prophet Ya'qūb ﷺ was not fooled for even one minute. He was deeply saddened by his sons' behavior. He knew that they had done something bad to Yūsuf ﷺ, and that they were lying to cover it up.

Tears of sorrow welled up in his eyes as he told his sons how ashamed he was of them. "You may think that these lies are the truth, but I will be patient and Allāh ﷻ will soon make the truth be known."[9]

Hurt by their jealous behavior, he turned and left them. Once alone, he prayed and prayed for Yūsuf's safe return. He asked Allāh ﷻ to give his missing son strength and courage while he was on his own. Many days and nights passed and still, there was no sign of Yūsuf ﷺ. Ya'qūb ﷺ continued to shed so many tears that he eventually became blind.

YŪSUF ﷺ IS FOUND

Every day, Yūsuf's ﷺ brothers went to the well to see if he was still there. Days passed, yet he remained at the bottom of the well. Yūsuf's brothers were beginning to wonder if anyone would *ever* find him. Finally, one day, as they watched from some distant trees, they saw a caravan of traders stop near the well. The travellers sent one of their men to fetch water. As the bucket dangled in front of Prophet Yūsuf ﷺ, he quickly seized the opportunity to climb into it. *Finally he would be freed*, he thought as he was brought up. The man was so surprised by the sight of Yūsuf ﷺ that he almost dropped the bucket back into the well! He rubbed his eyes in disbelief, but when he opened them, the boy was still there.

"Look what I have found," he called to his companions. When his fellow merchants came up to see, they were just as surprised. "This young man is so handsome that we will be able to sell him for a lot of money!"[10] They planned to take young Yūsuf ﷺ to Memphis, the capital of Egypt, where slave trade was very popular. There, they knew that they would be able to earn a hefty sum of money for the boy.

YŪSUF ﷺ AND THE GREAT 'AZĪZ

The merchants soon learned that Yūsuf ﷺ was a real treasure. Many wealthy people in Memphis wanted to buy him. It was obvious to all that Yūsuf ﷺ was not only strong and handsome, but very intelligent and polite. Each day, the price for Yūsuf ﷺ rose higher and higher. Finally, the ruler of the city, the 'Azīz, offered the largest amount of gold for him.

The 'Azīz took Yūsuf ﷺ home with him and showed him to his wife. "We will treat him well," said the 'Azīz, who was a very kind man. "Maybe having this boy in our home will be a blessing for us. Maybe we can even adopt him as our own son."[12]

Yūsuf ﷺ stayed with the 'Azīz for many years. He grew from a young boy to a strong and handsome man. He was also very pious, with a deep faith in

Allāh ﷻ. He was blessed with knowledge and wisdom. Like his father, he had the ability to interpret dreams. The 'Azīz was very kind to Yūsuf ﷺ and he cared for him as if he was a family member. He was impressed with Yūsuf's politeness and honesty.

Around the city, women would fall in love with Yūsuf ﷺ the moment they set eyes on him. He was so handsome that as soon as he entered the room, they would become speechless and forget what they were doing.

One woman fell in love with Yūsuf ﷺ more than all the other women, and that was the 'Azīz's very own wife! Whenever she saw him, her heart melted and she felt weak. One day, she could not hold herself back anymore, so she grabbed him and tried to kiss him. But Yūsuf ﷺ was too noble to do such a thing, so he pushed her way and told her to leave him alone.

This only made the 'Azīz's wife angry. "If you do not do what I tell you to, I will send you to jail!" she threatened.

Prophet Yūsuf ﷺ had such fine morals that he decided that he would rather go to jail than do something that would make Allāh ﷻ angry. He also respected the 'Azīz very much, and would never do anything to hurt him. Because of these reasons, he asked the 'Azīz to send him to jail so that he could escape his wife.[13]

YŪSUF'S TIME IN PRISON

Prophet Yūsuf ﷺ ended up going to jail for a crime that he did not commit. However, he knew that it was better than staying in the same house as the 'Azīz's wife.

Prophet Yūsuf ﷺ shared a jail cell with two young men. They were servants of the Fir'awn and had been thrown into jail for making him angry. It was not long before Prophet Yūsuf ﷺ became friends with them and enlightened them with his abundant knowledge. They were very impressed by the clarity with which he spoke and the wise things which he said. As the days and months passed, Yūsuf ﷺ also taught them about Allāh ﷻ and the importance of following the Straight Path.

One day, the two men approached Yūsuf ﷺ with very serious looks on their faces. "Oh, Yūsuf, I had a very strange dream," one said. "I dreamt that I was crushing grapes to make some wine."

"I, too, had a strange dream," said the other. "I dreamt that I was carrying bread on my head, and birds were eating from it. Can you tell us the meanings of these two dreams?"

"Come back to me tomorrow. *Inshā' Allāh*, I will tell you the meaning

of your dreams then, my friends," replied the Prophet ﷺ.[14]

The next morning, the two men returned to Yūsuf ﷺ for the interpretations of their dreams. Yūsuf ﷺ turned to the man who had dreamt of crushing grapes.

"You will be freed from jail and will live in the King's palace, where you will serve him wine." Then he turned toward the other inmate.

"You will die on a cross for your crime, my friend," he said sadly. "When you die, birds will eat from your head."[15]

As time passed, Yūsuf's predictions came true. One man was killed on a cross, and the other was set free. As the freed servant was leaving the prison, he thanked Prophet Yūsuf ﷺ for having given him guidance and knowledge. Yūsuf ﷺ reminded him to tell the King about him, so that perhaps he, too, could be set free.

His friend promised that he would. However, once he got out, he was so excited to be free that he forgot his promise to Yūsuf ﷺ. As a result, the Prophet ﷺ ended up staying in jail for many more years.[16]

THE KING'S DREAM

Many years later, the King of Egypt had a very strange dream. The next morning he called his advisors to tell them about it. "In my dream, I saw seven fat cows being eaten by seven skinny cows," said the King with a confused look on his face. "Then I saw seven green ears of corn and seven dry ears of corn. Can any of you tell me what this means?"[17]

His advisors thought long and hard, but could not understand the meaning of the dream. Suddenly, the king's wine server remembered Yūsuf ﷺ. He was ashamed that he had forgotten about his friend for so long. He hoped that now he could make up for his mistake.

"I know a way to find the meaning of your dream,"[18] he told the King. The King gave him permission to leave the palace and go find Prophet Yūsuf ﷺ. He went straight to the prison where he found Yūsuf still sitting in his cell.

He embraced his old friend and apologized for forgetting about him for so long. When Yūsuf ﷺ had forgiven him, he told the Prophet ﷺ about the King's dream.

Yūsuf ﷺ replied, "For seven years, you will plant many fields of corn. When you pick the corn, only eat a small portion of it. Save most of it for later, because there will be seven years of drought, when no rain will fall. Many people will be starving and looking for food, so it is important to save the corn from the seven good years to make sure that there is enough for everyone to eat.

After the seven years of drought pass, Allāh ﷻ will send lots of rain. There will be plenty of food to eat, and the people will make juices and oils and many other good things."[19]

Yūsuf's friend thanked him and promised that he would do all he could to release him from prison. He rushed back to the royal palace to inform the King of the interpretation. When the King heard what the servant had to say, he was grateful to have learned such valuable information.

"Bring this man to me," he instructed his servant. "I will make him my most trusted assistant."

The servant took the King's message back to Yūsuf ﷺ and let him know that he was now a free man. Although Yūsuf ﷺ was glad to be free at last, he was upset by the fact that people still did not know the truth about him and the 'Azīz's wife.

"Before I get out, go back to the King and ask about the lady who was after me,"[20] he said. Yūsuf ﷺ refused to leave the prison until his name was cleared of any wrongdoing.

The King sent for the wife of the 'Azīz. He asked her why Yūsuf ﷺ had gone to jail and what had really happened. The 'Azīz's wife was suddenly overcome by guilt for what she had done to Yūsuf ﷺ. "I was wrong. I was the one who tried to kiss him," she confessed. "He did not do anything wrong because he respected Allāh ﷻ and the 'Azīz, who was his master. Yūsuf ﷺ is an honorable and righteous man." When everyone heard this, they realized that he had been innocent all along.

When Prophet Yūsuf ﷺ was freed from prison, he immediately went to work for the King. As time passed, the King became very impressed with his honesty and hard work. He appointed Yūsuf ﷺ to be in charge of the storehouses, where the crops and food would be stored for the drought.[21] It was his job to make sure that enough food was being saved for the bad years to come. This was a very big responsibility but Yūsuf ﷺ was a hard worker. He was always fair and respectful to the farmers who brought their crops to the storehouse, and it was not long before his reputation became widely known.

The storehouses overflowed with corn and other grains by the time the seven years of good harvest had passed. Then, as if by magic, the rain stopped coming. The land became dry and dusty, and the ground cracked under the extreme heat. The plants and vegetation withered and died. Throughout the region, the drought depleted harvests and food supplies dwindled. People began to panic about the possibility of starvation. However, because of his careful planning, Yūsuf ﷺ made sure that everyone had enough to eat.

Word of the King's surplus of food spread quickly. Soon, caravans and

travelers from every corner of the region were coming to Egypt to buy food. The King was extremely proud of his intelligent and gifted advisor. Because of him, the kingdom was making money even in a time of drought. Clearly, Yūsuf ﷺ was a special person.

A STRANGE REUNION

It was common for people to travel from near and far to buy food from Yūsuf ﷺ. In time, he had seen people from just about every corner of Arabia, and it was rare that anything surprised him - except for the one thing he was least expecting.

One day, as he presided over the storehouses, he looked up to see a caravan arriving. He approached to greet the travellers, and his heart leapt into his throat when he saw their faces. He could not believe who was standing before him. Even after so many years he could still recognize them. *They were his brothers!*

Yūsuf's heart stood still and he shook his head in disbelief. However, he quickly regained his composure and greeted them respectfully. They returned the greeting and began to talk business. It was clear that they did not recognize him.[22] How could they? They had sold him as a slave when he was just a boy. Now he was one of the most powerful men in the land. They never could have imagined this to be possible.

Seeing his brothers reminded Yūsuf ﷺ of his father and closest brother, Bin Yāmīn. He could not help but feel sad at the thought that they still had no idea where he was.

Despite the pain he was feeling, he did not tell his brothers who he was.

He treated them kindly and respectfully, and sold them corn at a very fair price. But as they left, he could not help but make one request.

"Next time you come, you must bring your youngest brother, who has a different mother than you,"[23] he said.

His brothers were surprised at this peculiar request. They not only wondered what significance their youngest brother Bin Yāmīn had, but they also wondered how Yūsuf ﷺ could have known that they even had a younger brother from a different mother! They looked at each other, trying not to act too surprised, and then nodded to Yūsuf ﷺ.

"We will ask our father to let him come with us next time,"[24] they assured him.

When his brothers were not looking, Yūsuf ﷺ ordered one of his assistants to secretly return the goods that they had used to purchase the corn.

The assistant quietly went to their caravan and replaced the goods into their saddlebags.[25] When he finished, he quietly returned to Yūsuf ﷺ to let him know that he had accomplished the task.

THE BROTHERS RETURN HOME

When Yūsuf's brothers returned home, they lovingly greeted their blind father. They did not know how to tell their father about Yūsuf's strange request to bring Bin Yāmīn with them next time. Prophet Ya'qūb ﷺ knew that they had done something terrible to Yūsuf ﷺ, so it would be nearly impossible for him to agree to let them take Bin Yāmīn. Finally, one of the brothers spoke up.

"Father," he began carefully. "We cannot get any more goods unless we take Bin Yāmīn with us. The director of the storage houses made that very clear. Please send him with us."[26] They could see the disturbed look on Prophet Ya'qūb's face, so they tried to reassure him. "We promise that he will be safe with us. We will take very good care of him."

Prophet Ya'qūb ﷺ clearly did not like the idea. "Remember what happened when I trusted you with Yūsuf ﷺ? I cannot trust you with Bin Yāmīn,"[27] he said shaking his head sadly.

They knew that their father had a right to mistrust them, but they had no idea how to convince him that they really would protect Bin Yāmīn. Perhaps they would be able to convince him later, they thought. They opened their saddlebags to remove and store the grain they had bought. To their surprise, they found that someone had secretly returned the goods they had used to purchase the grains.

"Look, Father!" they exclaimed. "What more can we ask for? Someone has returned our goods to us. Now we can return and buy even more. Please let us go with Bin Yāmīn and we will get a full load of food."[28]

Prophet Ya'qūb ﷺ knew the family would soon be in dire need of more food. He really had no choice but to let them take Bin Yāmīn when they went back.

"I will not send Bin Yāmīn with you until you promise, in the name of Allah ﷻ, to protect him with your lives. You must bring him back to me unless you are made absolutely powerless to do so," he warned.[29]

The brothers solemnly swore to protect and care for Bin Yāmīn. When the time came for them to return to Egypt, they packed their things and prepared their caravan.

Before they left, Ya'qūb ﷺ advised his sons: "You should not all enter the city through the same gate or leave through the same gate." He knew that such a large group of travellers might draw the attention of some thieves or troublemakers. All eleven brothers agreed to do as their father had instructed.

"Put your trust in Allāh ﷻ,"[30] Ya'qūb ﷺ advised his sons as they began their journey. As he heard the footsteps of the camels dwindle into the desert night, he thought of his dear Bin Yāmīn and prayed for his safety. He, too, would have to put his faith in Allāh ﷻ.

THE FAMILY REUNION

When Prophet Yūsuf ﷺ saw his brothers approaching, he rushed to them and greeted them warmly. He could hardly contain his joy at finally seeing Bin Yāmīn. His younger brother had grown so big and handsome over the years. Prophet Yūsuf ﷺ invited his brothers to join him for dinner and they happily

agreed. After all, he had been kind enough to return their goods to them on their previous visit. They sat in a circle and feasted on delicious foods and Prophet Yūsuf ﷺ made it a point to sit next to Bin Yāmīn. He waited for the conversation to break into little groups, and then seized the opportunity to speak to his brother.

"Bin Yāmīn," he said quickly and quietly. "I am your brother, Yūsuf. Do not be sad about the things our brothers have done."[31]

When Bin Yāmīn heard this, his face beamed with joy and his heart leaped with relief. Knowing that Yūsuf ﷺ did not want his brothers to know the truth, he made every effort to fight back the desire to cry and laugh at the same time. He wanted to embrace his long lost brother so badly that it hurt. But instead, he quietly let Yūsuf ﷺ know that his secret was safe.

Prophet Yūsuf ﷺ planned to keep Bin Yāmīn with him. So the next day, as he was filling his brothers' bags with grain, he hid the King's golden cup in Bin Yāmīn's saddlebag.

As the brothers thanked Yūsuf ﷺ for his hospitality and started on their return journey, Yūsuf ﷺ suddenly called out, "Stop that caravan! One of them is a thief!"[32]

The brothers turned to Yūsuf ﷺ with shock and bewilderment. "What has been stolen?"[33] they asked in confusion.

"We are missing the King's golden cup!" exclaimed Yūsuf ﷺ. "Whoever finds it will be given the reward of a load of corn!"[34]

"By Allāh!" his brothers swore. "We know that it is wrong to steal and we are not thieves."[35]

But even as they protested, the King's servants began searching the caravan. When Bin Yāmīn's saddlebag was opened, the cup was found and held

up for all to see.

The brothers saw this and became afraid of what the King would do to Bin Yāmīn. They remembered their promise to their father. They knew that this would break his heart.

"Our father is already old and sick," they pleaded with Yūsuf ﷺ. "He loves Bin Yāmīn very much. He will suffer even more if you arrest his favorite son. Please, we beg you, take one of us instead."[36] It was clear that they sincerely wanted to protect Bin Yāmīn and this warmed Yūsuf's heart. His brothers had definitely changed over the years.

Still, Prophet Yūsuf ﷺ said, "Allāh ﷻ forbids me to take another person other than the one who had the cup. It would be wrong for me to do that."[37]

Despite constant pleading with Yūsuf ﷺ, the brothers realized that there was no hope of convincing him to release Bin Yāmīn. The oldest brother decided that he would stay with him.

"We made a promise to our father, in the name of Allāh ﷻ, that we would watch over and protect our youngest brother," he told his siblings. "I will not leave from here until Father tells me to come home or Allāh ﷻ guides me to leave. All of you go back home and tell Father that Bin Yāmīn had to stay in Egypt because he stole something. Tell him that we did not see it happen so we were unable to stop him."[38]

The nine brothers sadly returned to their father and told him the story with genuine tears in their eyes. When he heard his sons' story, Ya'qūb ﷺ became greatly disturbed.

"You are not telling me the truth." Tears welled up in his eyes. "I know that Bin Yāmīn would not steal. I must be patient, and Allāh ﷻ will bring both of my sons back to me."[39]

The brothers became angry that he would not forget about Yūsuf ﷺ, and they quickly lashed out, "By Allāh! Will you please forget about him! Forget him before you become so sick that you die!"[40]

Prophet Ya'qūb ﷺ turned back to face his sons, his voice growing angry. "I have only told Allāh ﷻ about my grief. He knows things that you do not know." Prophet Ya'qūb ﷺ had faith in Allāh ﷻ. He knew that Yūsuf ﷺ was still alive and that some day he would be reunited with his son.

"Oh, my sons," he ordered them. "Return to Egypt and find Yūsuf and his brother. We must never give up hope of Allāh's mercy. We must always have faith in Him."[41]

Obeying their father's instructions, all nine of them returned to Egypt. Upon their arrival, they went straight to Prophet Yūsuf ﷺ.

"Sadness and pain has come to our family," they said to him. "We only have a small amount of money left. Will you give us a full load of corn for whatever we have? This will be a charity."[42]

Yūsuf ﷺ could hear the despair in their voice and see the distress in their eyes. Although it pained him to see his brothers like this, he wanted them to realize how cruel they had been to him and Bin Yāmīn.

After a moment of silence, he asked them, "Do you remember how you treated Yūsuf ﷺ and his brother?"[43]

As soon as he had asked the question, the brothers realized who he was. For a moment, nothing was said as they stared in wide-eyed disbelief. Their mouths hung open but no sounds came out. It seemed much too absurd to be possible. Yūsuf ﷺ could see the shock on their faces.

"Are...are you really Yūsuf ﷺ?" stuttered one of the brothers as the silence was broken.

"I am Yūsuf and this is my brother Bin Yāmīn," he replied with a gentle smile. "Allāh ﷻ has been good to us. Those who are righteous and patient are always blessed."[44]

"Oh Yūsuf, what a terrible thing we have done to you," they moaned painfully. His brothers were so overcome by guilt that they hung their heads in shame. They wept and begged him for forgiveness for what they had done.

But Prophet Yūsuf ﷺ had no desire to punish them. He approached them gently and kindly embraced them.

"Do not feel bad, my dear brothers," he consoled them. "Today, Allāh ﷻ will forgive you. Now go! Hurry back home! Take this shirt of mine and lay it on my father's face. The sorrow will leave his eyes and he will be able to see again. Then bring the whole family back to Egypt with you!"[45] he exclaimed excitedly.

The brothers each took turns embracing and kissing Yūsuf ﷺ, and they promised that they would never leave him again. Then they quickly turned their caravan around and headed home to share the wonderful news with their father.

As they made their way across the desert, headed towards Palestine, Ya'qūb ﷺ waited patiently at home. As his sons neared home, the elderly Prophet ﷺ suddenly sat up and leaned his head back, inhaling deeply through his nose. A gentle smile crossed his aged face.

"I smell the scent of Yūsuf in the air,"[46] he said softly.

Those who were around him were skeptical. "You are thinking of the past. This is a sign of your old age."[47]

However, Ya'qūb ﷺ knew in his heart that Yūsuf ﷺ was alive and well. He knew that when his sons arrived, they would bring some good news.

When the brothers finally arrived, they burst into the house and rushed to lay the shirt on Ya'qūb's face. Prophet Ya'qūb ﷺ felt the warmth of the material on his eyes and could smell the musky scent of Yūsuf ﷺ. When he opened his eyes, he could see again! He looked around the room, at the family members whom he had lived with, but not seen for so many years. He opened his arms to them and they rushed to embrace him.

Yūsuf's brothers had been through so much emotion and so many surprises in so little time that they were overwhelmed. They did not try to hold back the tears that streamed down their faces. Never before had they felt so much shame, elation and wonder all at once.

"Oh Father!" they cried. "Ask Allāh ﷻ to forgive us for the bad things that we have done."[49] When Ya'qūb ﷺ saw the genuine sorrow and regret on his sons' faces, he immediately prayed for their forgiveness.

TOGETHER AT LAST

The whole family packed their belongings and bid farewell to their neighbors and friends. They formed a large caravan and headed westward towards Egypt. When they finally arrived, Yūsuf ﷺ received them with tears of joy. He gave all his brothers new homes and invited his parents to stay with him. As Yūsuf ﷺ stood proudly in front of his family, reunited at last, his parents and eleven brothers prostrated before him to show their thankfulness to Allāh ﷻ.

Yūsuf ﷺ remembered the dream that he had when he was a young boy. In his dream, he had seen eleven stars and the sun and the moon all bowing down before him.

"O Father," he said. "My childhood dream has come true. It is Allāh ﷻ

Who has made it come true. He has shown me great kindness. He took me out of prison. And today, He has brought our family together again and He has made peace between my brothers and me!"[50]

Prophet Yūsuf ﷺ turned to Allāh ﷻ in prayer.

"O Lord!" he prayed. "You have given me some power, and taught me the meanings of dreams and events. O Allāh, You have created the Heavens and the Earth, and you are my Protector and Friend in this world and in the Hereafter. Let me live my whole life as one who is obedient to You."[51]

Yūsuf ﷺ then turned to his family as they rushed to embrace him in tearful joy.

Prophet Shu'aib عليه السلام

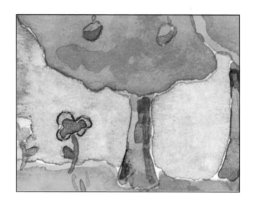

Prophet Shu'aib ﷺ was born into the tribe of Madyan many centuries before Prophet Mūsa ﷺ. Shu'aib ﷺ came from a very noble and respected family. His great-great grandfather, also named Madyan, was the son of Prophet Ibrāhīm ﷺ, and his wife was Keturah. The people of Madyan lived in Ḥijāz, the land of Prophet Ibrāhīm ﷺ, close to the eastern bank of the Red Sea.

Madyan was a bright and sunny land with waterfalls and orchards filled with trees that grew delicious fruits. An abundance of fragrant flowers perfumed the air. The people of Madyan were traders. Allāh ﷻ had blessed them with the presence of two waterways: the Red Sea and the Gulf of Aqabah. These waters were very helpful to the traders because they would use them to transport their goods to other areas for trade.

At first, the tribe of Madyan was very small. Then, Allāh ﷻ blessed them with many children. Soon the people of Madyan formed a lively, bustling city. As they grew in number, they also grew in wealth and success. They continued to build larger buildings and expand their business, taking great pride in what they had accomplished. But as the years passed, they began to lose sight of what was important in life. They forgot the teachings of Islām that Prophet Ibrāhīm ﷺ had brought to them. They did not thank Allāh ﷻ for all the blessings that He had given them.

As Shu'aib ﷺ grew up, he watched the people around him and he became disturbed by what he saw. His people were drinking, gambling and stealing from one another. When they did business, they cheated their customers by giving them less than what they paid for. Instead of worshipping Allāh ﷻ, they prayed to idols which they had made with their own hands. The people

were so lost that they did not even realize that what they were doing was wrong. They did not realize that all of their riches and wealth were gifts from Allāh ﷻ. They thought that it was purely by chance that they lived in such a beautiful and scenic land.

Shuʻaib ﷺ continued to pray that his people would turn towards Allāh ﷻ and see the truth. When he became an adult, Allāh ﷻ made him a prophet and ordered him to bring the people of Madyan back to the Straight Path. When he found out the news, Shuʻaib was full of joy and eagerness. Nothing in the world could be better than to serve the call of Allāh ﷻ. Prophet Shuʻaib ﷺ began his task immediately.

"O my people!" he called to them. "Worship Allāh, Who is your only Lord. Give up these idols which are deaf, dumb and blind. They can do nothing for you."

He then advised them to act in a fair and responsible manner, saying, "Stop cheating people by giving them fewer goods than they pay for. Stop taking away the rights of the people. Stop making others afraid to worship Allāh ﷻ and do not stop them from turning towards Him in prayer. Remember what happened to those who refused to believe in Allah ﷻ."[1]

Allāh ﷻ had blessed Shu'aib ﷺ with a beautiful and melodic voice. He spoke in a clear and gentle tone, using rich and poetic language. People would come just to hear his voice as he preached. Many great scholars have given him the name of *Khatīb al-Anbiyā'* which means the "Voice of the Prophets."

Despite his beautiful voice and the logical Message he brought, many people still refused to follow Prophet Shu'aib ﷺ. They did not like what he had to say and they simply refused to change their ways. They did not think that obeying Allāh ﷻ was important.

"O Shu'aib!" they shouted. "Does your Lord teach you that we must give up all the idols that our grandfathers worshiped before us? Why does He tell you that we cannot do what we want with our own goods?"[2]

Shu'aib ﷺ always responded to their screaming complaints in a polite and dignified manner. He spoke calmly and kindly to show them that he really cared about them. He knew that many of them were wonderful people who had simply lost touch with the truth.

"O my people," he said. "Think about the message that I bring you. I do not want to fight with you. I only wish that you would stop doing the evil things that will ruin you. I want nothing from you except that you obey Allāh ﷻ." Unfortunately, the more he talked to them and the more he pointed out the error of their ways, the angrier they became.

"Do not let your hatred of me cause you to disbelieve in the message that I bring," he pleaded. "If you do not believe in Allāh ﷻ, you will be punished just like the people of Nūḥ ﷺ, the people of Hūd ﷺ, the people of Ṣāliḥ ﷺ and the people of Lūṭ ﷺ were punished."[3]

"We do not understand what you are talking about, Shu'aib," the people said rudely. "You are a weakling. If you were not from the family of Madyan we would stone you. We are certainly much more powerful than you."[4]

Although most of the town's people were not receptive to his teachings, eventually Shu'aib's efforts began to pay off. Slowly, people became convinced that he really was a Prophet of Allāh ﷻ and that he brought them a true Message. Day by day, his followers began to increase in number as they examined the problems within their society. They stopped gambling and cheating. They gave up their idols and accepted Allāh ﷻ as their only Lord.

The leaders of Madyan watched all this in growing fear. Prophet Shu'aib ﷺ was teaching his people to stand up for justice and to speak out against oppression and the leaders of Madyan did not like it one bit. They felt that Shu'aib ﷺ was a threat to their power and influence over the people. They knew that if he continued to gain followers, they would be in serious trouble. When they could no longer stand it, the *Kuffār* decided to terrorize the believers.

"If you continue to follow that crazy man, we will kill you!" they threatened. Sometimes they would block the streets by standing in front of the believers and not allowing them to pass. When others were not around, they would grab Shu'aib's followers and beat them. They believed that their scare tactics would shake the faith of the righteous. "We will take everything away from you if you continue this nonsense," they warned.[5]

Despite the *Kuffār's* constant pressure, Prophet Shu'aib's followers continued to meet and spread his message. As the days passed, the treatment from the *Kuffār* became even worse. The *Kuffār* were now openly harassing the believers, telling them to leave town.

It hurt Prophet Shu'aib ﷺ to see his followers suffer. "If some of you believe in this message that I have brought from Allāh ﷻ, and some of you do not believe in it, just wait and be patient," he consoled them. "Allāh ﷻ will show you who has made the best choice."[6]

Prophet Shu'aib's wise words were ignored by the sinister people of Madyan. Even members of his own tribe began to threaten to banish him from the city.

They said, "Oh Shu'aib! We will drive you and your followers out of this city if you do not give up preaching Islām."[7]

Finally, Allāh ﷻ became angry with the people of Madyan. He had given them many chances to change their ways. He had sent a kind and gentle prophet to them, who was of their own people. It was clear that nothing would make them see the Truth. The only thing to do was to punish them the way other people before them had been punished for rejecting the Truth.

One night, as the people slept soundly, a giant earthquake shook the city. It started as a low rumbling, but it soon elevated into a booming crash as the earth suddenly came to life. The ground began to shake violently, rocking back and forth. Along the ground, cracks appeared and widened into deep craters that swallowed entire homes. The non believers were thrown out of their beds by the force of the quake. They bounced uncontrollably off the walls and floors, as their houses collapsed on top of them. Many of them realized that this was the punishment of Allāh ﷻ that Prophet Shuʿaib ﷺ had promised would come. But by that time, it was far too late.

Although Prophet Shuʿaib ﷺ was very kindhearted, he told his followers not to grieve for those who had died in the earthquake.

"I brought them a clear and pure message from Allāh ﷻ. It was a message for their own good. I cannot feel sorry for them or cry for them since they continued to refuse the Truth," he explained.[8]

Prophet Shu'aib ﷺ was ordered by Allāh ﷻ to take his people and move to a nearby country, where they lived happily for many years. In their new land, they were free to gather and learn from their wise and insightful Prophet ﷺ. They knew that this community of believers was the perfect environment to raise their children to become respectful and fair adults. May Allāh ﷻ bless them for their efforts and strength.

Prophet Mūsa ﷺ

Prophet Mūsa ﷺ came from a noble family of prophets. His great-grandfather was Prophet Ya'qūb ﷺ and his grandfather was Prophet Yūsuf ﷺ. Like other prophets throughout history, he was sent to the Banī Isrā'il which means the "Children of Isrā'il ." The Children of Isrā'il , also known as Israelites, were descendants of Prophet Isḥāq ﷺ and Prophet Ibrāhīm ﷺ. Isrā'il means "Servant of Allāh" and this was the name that Allāh ﷻ had given to Prophet Ya'qūb ﷺ.

Prophet Ya'qūb ﷺ had twelve sons, one of which was Prophet Yūsuf ﷺ. Prophet Yūsuf ﷺ and his brothers settled in the land of Egypt, and their children were called the Bani Isrā'il . After Prophet Yūsuf ﷺ died, the Children of Isrā'il were made into slaves by the Egyptian kings. An Egyptian king was called a Pharaoh or *Fir'awn*.

The Egyptian Pharaohs did not like the Banī Isrā'il, because they were the descendants of Prophet Ibrāhīm ﷺ and were regarded as an inferior race. The priests and wise men of Egypt had told the Pharaohs that, many years ago, Allāh ﷻ had promised Ibrāhīm ﷺ to make some of his children kings and prophets. The kings of Egypt wanted to stop this from happening. They thought and thought and finally, they came up with plan.

They decided to kill all the baby boys born to Israelite parents. This way, no Israelite boy would grow up to fight the kings. The Pharaohs sent messengers throughout the land to find all the women of Bani Isrā'il about to have babies. The Pharaoh's men would then wait to see whether a son or a daughter was born. If it was a son, he was taken away and killed.

This practice went on for several years. Each year, all the newborn baby boys were taken from their mothers and killed. Soon, however, the

Pharaohs realized that if they killed all the baby boys, there would be no more slaves left. They did not like this idea, so they decided to only kill baby boys every other year.

Even though the Bani Isrā'il had been Muslims a long time ago, many of them had forgotten the teachings of their prophets. They forgot to worship only Allāh ﷻ. Many of them began to worship the cow and other gods of the Pharaohs. Finally, Allāh ﷻ decided to send a prophet to save the Banī Isrā'il from the *Fir'awn* and to show them the Straight Path of Islām. He chose Prophet Mūsa ﷺ.

At the time of Prophet Mūsa's birth, the most evil *Fir'awn* ever was ruling Egypt. His wickedness was known throughout the land. Every other year, he would kill all the baby boys born to families of Bani Isrā'il. He was afraid that

Allāh's promise to Prophet Ibrāhīm ﷺ would come true during his lifetime, and that he would be thrown out of his own kingdom.

BABY MŪSA IS SAVED

Mūsa ﷺ was born in a year in which baby boys were being killed. His mother was terrified that *Fir'awn*'s men would take her baby away and kill him. Although she was able to hide him for a while, she knew that it was only a matter of time before *Fir'awn*'s soldiers found him. Every night, for three months, she prayed to Allāh ﷻ to save her baby. Allāh ﷻ had a special plan for the blessed infant and He was going to make sure that he was safe.

One night, Allāh ﷻ told her to put Mūsa ﷺ into a basket and place the basket in the Nile River.[1] Allāh ﷻ promised to protect the baby and return him to her soon. Mūsa's mother was comforted by Allāh's promise so she did as she was told.

The next day, she wrapped her lovely son in a blanket and held him close, kissing him lovingly before laying him tenderly in the basket. She quietly made her way to the shores of the Nile River and placed the basket into it. The flowing waters delicately pulled the basket into the current, where it floated gently down the Nile. Mūsa's mother prayed to Allāh ﷻ to keep him safe. Then she instructed her daughter to follow the basket to see what happened.

Mūsa's sister carefully made her way through the tall grass and brush on the banks of the river, moving swiftly to keep the basket in sight. Suddenly, she came to a stop and held her breath as she watched the basket float straight into the *Fir'awn*'s garden! She was powerless to do anything. Her mother had placed Mūsa ﷺ in the water to protect him from the *Fir'awn* and he ended up right at the *Fir'awn*'s doorstep! *What was going to happen?*

Some of *Fir'awn*'s servants were bathing in the river when one of them

spied the basket. They quickly made their way towards it and pulled it out of the water. They took it directly to *Fir'awn*'s wife, Queen Asiyāh 🌹. As everyone crowded around her, she opened the lid of the basket. What she saw made her gasp in disbelief. Inside was a tiny baby, looking back at her in wonder.

When Queen Asiyāh 🌹 looked into the baby's deep eyes she could not help but hold the child close to her. He was the most beautiful baby she had ever seen. *Fir'awn*'s guards heard the commotion and saw all the people gathered around the Queen. When they saw the baby, they rushed to take him from Queen Asiyāh 🌹. Sensing that it was a child, from the Bani Isrā'il, they wanted to kill it, but she stopped them.

"One little boy is not going to increase the power of the Banī Isrā'il," she scolded them.

As she held Baby Mūsa 🌹 and looked down into his tiny face, her heart melted. She rushed to show her husband the baby. Queen Asiyāh ﷺ knew that her husband did not like baby boys, but she thought that if he saw how cute this one was, he would change his mind.

"Maybe we can raise him as our own son," she said to her husband as he looked at the quiet infant.[2]

Fir'awn was not very happy about letting the Israelite child live, but when he saw how much his wife liked the baby, he decided to let her keep him. What harm could one more Israelite child cause? Queen Asiyāh ﷺ was so happy that she embraced her husband and hurried away with the baby in her arms.

Meanwhile, Mūsa's sister was hiding and watching from a distance. She breathed a sigh of relief when she saw that the Queen had not let the guards kill her little brother. She continued to watch curiously as the Queen handed Mūsa ﷺ to a woman. She then saw the woman attempt to feed the infant. Mūsa ﷺ

began to cry, letting out a piercing wail. It was clear that the baby was hungry, but for some reason he would not take this woman's milk.

Queen Asiyāh ﷺ became nervous. She did not have any children of her own, and she did not know what to do. She wanted so desperately for the child to stop his crying. She immediately sent some of her servants to the marketplace to see if they could find another woman who would feed Mūsa ﷺ. Mūsa's sister quietly followed them to the marketplace.

When they were far away from *Fir'awn*'s palace, she stepped forward and said, "Shall I take you to the house of a woman who will feed him? She will take care of him for you. Her family will be very kind to him."[3]

The servants quickly agreed because they could see that the Queen was getting desperate. They told Mūsa's sister to bring the woman to the palace. She rushed home with a big smile across her face to tell her mother the good news.

When Mūsa's mother heard the story, she hurried to the palace and she swept baby Mūsa into her arms. He immediately stopped crying and started to drink her milk. Queen Asiyāh ﷺ truly loved the baby and she was overjoyed to see him drinking the milk of this strange woman. The Queen begged Mūsa's mother to stay at the palace and nurse the baby. However, Mūsa's mother refused the Queen's offer because she had other children at home that needed her. Finally, the two women agreed that the baby would go back with his mother. It was also agreed that he would be brought to the palace whenever the Queen wanted to see him. Thus, Allāh's promise to Mūsa's mother was fulfilled and he was safely returned to her.

MŪSA ﷺ BECOMES A MAN

As the years passed, Mūsa ﷺ grew to be a handsome and strong young man. Allāh ﷻ blessed him with a happy childhood. He was treated like a prince in the house of *Fir'awn*. He had a special place in the heart of Queen Asiyāh ﵂ and the rest of the family. Even the servants became attached to the young boy who showed them as much respect as he did to the Queen and the *Fir'awn*.

In his own home, his mother taught him about Allāh ﷻ and the religion of his grandfathers. She told him how Allāh ﷻ had saved him from *Fir'awn*. As Mūsa ﷺ grew older, he saw the cruel way in which *Fir'awn*'s people treated the Bani Isrā'il people. He knew that these slaves were his own people, and it pained him to know that they were in such a horrible situation. He knew that it was only by a miracle of Allāh ﷻ that he himself had not been killed by *Fir'awn* when he was born. The more Mūsa ﷺ saw his people being tortured, the more dedicated he became to the idea of setting them free.

One day, as Mūsa ﷺ was passing through the city, he saw two men fighting. One of the men belonged to Bani Isrā'il and the other was one of *Fir'awn*'s own men. The man had a bad reputation and was known to be a troublemaker, but Mūsa ﷺ did not know this.

The man saw Mūsa ﷺ and pleaded, "Oh Mūsa, please help me." Mūsa ﷺ felt sorry for him and he was angered by the constant persecution of the Bani Isrā'il by *Fir'awn*'s men. Without thinking, he ran up to them and struck *Fir'awn*'s man on the head. The man grunted and instantly collapsed to the ground. Mūsa ﷺ had killed him! Mūsa ﷺ stepped back, shaking his head in disbelief at what he had done. He had only been trying to help. He had not meant to kill anyone. He knew that he should not have become so angry.

"This is the work of <u>Sh</u>ai̇ṭān. <u>Sh</u>ai̇ṭān is an enemy that leads people to the wrong path,"[4] he said sadly as he lowered his head in shame.

He also knew that if the *Fir'awn* found out about this, he would become very angry and punish not only Mūsa ﷺ, but all of the people of Bani Isrā'il. He prayed to Allāh ﷻ to forgive him for his deed.

"O my Lord!" Mūsa ﷺ prayed. "I have made a great mistake. Please forgive me!" He made a promise to Allāh ﷻ that he would never help someone who was only trying to make trouble.

Allāh ﷻ knew that Mūsa ﷺ had made an honest mistake and that he was really sorry for what he had done, so He forgave him.[5] The next morning, when Mūsa ﷺ went into the city, he was very careful. He looked around for *Fir'awn*'s guards to come and arrest him for his crime. However, there were no guards to be seen. He felt comforted by this and continued on his way.

"Help! Help!" he suddenly heard someone calling. Mūsa ﷺ went to investigate. He saw that it was the same man who had been fighting the day before. Once again, he was fighting another one of *Fir'awn*'s men. Mūsa ﷺ was smarter this time. He knew that the Israelite man had probably started the fight in the first place.

"You are nothing but a trouble maker. Here you are again fighting with someone else. You must be a person who has lost the righteous path," he told him. Then he made his way towards the both of them to separate them. When the Israelite saw Mūsa ﷺ approaching with a look of displeasure on his face, he became afraid that he would be beaten, and perhaps instantly killed, as the man had been the previous day.

"O Mūsa," he begged. "Do you want to kill me like you killed that other man yesterday? Are you just a cruel person or are you someone who desires to make peace between two people?"[6] *Fir'awn's* man instantly stepped back, staring in disbelief at Mūsa ﷺ. The news of the murdered man had spread throughout town but, until now, nobody had known who was responsible. Before Mūsa ﷺ could say anything, the man was running towards the palace, rushing to inform everyone who the murderer was.

Mūsa ﷺ did not know whether he should flee Egypt or stay and hope that the situation would simply calm down. He spent the whole day weighing his options and thinking of alternatives, when a man came running up to him, out of breath. He was coming to warn Mūsa ﷺ.

"Hurry, hurry!" he yelled excitedly. "The chiefs of *Fir'awn* are having a meeting and they are planing to kill you. You must leave this city at once. Trust me, I am your friend."[7] One look at the man's face told Mūsa ﷺ that he was very serious. It was no longer safe for Mūsa ﷺ in the palace or in the city. He knew he must leave right away. He looked at the land he had been raised in; the land of his people, the land of the Queen who had cared for him; and the land of the mother who had raised him and taught him about Allāh ﷻ. Because of his anger the other day, he was now forced to leave this very dear land or face certain death.

Quickly gathering a few belongings, Mūsa ﷺ left Egypt. As he fled, he prayed to Allāh ﷻ to help him. "O my Lord! Save me from these wrongdoing people."[8]

As he secretly made his way across the desert, he turned to look at his beloved place of birth one last time. He knew that now it would be even harder to save his people from the tyrannical *Fir'awn* and his evil men. He promised himself that no matter what happened, he would return one day to save his people.

MŪSA ﷺ FINDS A HOME WITH THE PEOPLE OF MADYAN

Mūsa ﷺ decided that he would be safe in Madyan, a city in Arabia. This was a place many hundreds of miles away, across the Gulf of Suez and the Sinai Desert. He knew that *Fir'awn*'s men would not follow him all the way there.

After many days of travel, Mūsa ﷺ reached Madyan. He was hot and tired from his long journey. His hair was ragged and his skin was bronzed from the glare of the sun. His clothes were dusty and worn. Just as he was being overcome by feelings of homesickness and loneliness, he came across an oasis with a well of cool, sweet water and palm trees to shade him from the blazing desert sun. With a sense of joy and relief, he made his way towards the oasis.

As Mūsa ﷺ rested, he noticed a number of shepherds drawing water from the well to water their flock. They were pushing and shoving for position, each man trying to get water before everyone else. Behind the shepherds, some girls stood patiently, waiting their turn for the water. He thought that it was quite rude of the shepherds not to let the girls go ahead of them.

Mūsa ﷺ walked up to the girls and asked, "What is the matter?"

"We cannot give water to our sheep until the men move out of the way. We do not have any men to help us because our father is old and weak."[9] Mūsa ﷺ was a kindhearted man and he felt sorry for the girls. He offered to fetch the water for them. He grabbed their buckets and made his way into the crowd of swarming men. Within minutes, he emerged carrying full buckets of water for the girls. He placed the buckets at their feet and wished them well. Then, he politely smiled and walked away.

When the sisters reached home, they told their elderly father about the

young man who had so kindly helped them. According to some, their father was none other than Prophet Shu'aib ﷺ. There are some who believe their father was an old priest in the family of Prophet Shu'aib ﷺ. Prophet Shu'aib ﷺ had a noble heart so he told his daughters to go back and invite the man to their house. The sisters hurried back to the oasis and found Mūsa ﷺ still resting in the shade. One of the sisters politely went up to him and invited him to come back with them. "My father invites you to our home. He wants to reward you for helping us."[10] Mūsa ﷺ was surprised because he had not helped them for a reward or a favor. He had only wanted to please Allāh ﷻ.

Mūsa ﷺ ended up spending many days with Prophet Shu'aib ﷺ and his family, during which time he became good friends with the elderly Prophet. Mūsa ﷺ told him about his life in Egypt, the *Fir'awn*'s beautiful palace and how his people had been made into slaves. Mūsa ﷺ explained to him how he had accidentally killed one of *Fir'awn*'s men and was forced to flee Egypt. Shu'aib ﷺ kindly listened to Mūsa's stories. "Don't be afraid," he reassured Mūsa ﷺ. "You are safe from those evil people while you are here with us."[11]

One day, one of the girls went to her father and asked him to give Mūsa ﷺ some work. She thought that Mūsa ﷺ was a very strong and honest man and he would take good care of their business.[12] Prophet Shu'aib ﷺ was surprised by his daughter's request. "How do you know that he is strong and honest?" he asked her.

"I know that he is strong because I saw the way he fetched the water for us in the biggest bucket. I know that he is honest and noble because when we went to invite him to our home, he kept his eyes down and did not stare at us."

Shu'aib ﷺ was very pleased with his daughter's clever reply and he invited Mūsa ﷺ to stay and work for them. "I would like you to marry one of my daughters, if you will stay and work for me for eight or ten years, he told Mūsa ﷺ. I will treat you kindly and, *Inshā' Allāh*, you will see that I am a righteous person."[13]

Mūsa ﷺ had grown close to the generous Prophet and his daughters. He felt he had another family with these noble people. Therefore, he gladly agreed to Shu'aib's request and married one of his daughters. They stayed with him for ten years, during which time Mūsa ﷺ worked for him in a dedicated and loving manner.

THE HOLY VALLEY

After several years of loving service to his father-in-law, Mūsa ﷺ was ready to take his family and move on. With tears in their eyes, they said goodbye to the Prophet ﷺ and the rest of his family. They set out into the desert with blessings and prayers from Shu'aib ﷺ and his family.

They travelled for many days and nights. It was a difficult journey which covered dangerous and rocky terrain. The blazing sun beat down on them during the day, and the nights were chilly and uncomfortable.

One night, Mūsa ﷺ saw a strange sight. In the distance, he spotted a burning fire. Perhaps he and his family were not the only people around after all!

"Wait here," Mūsa ﷺ told his wife. "I see a fire burning over there. Maybe I can find out what it is and bring you a firebrand to warm yourself."[14] Mūsa ﷺ left his family in a safe spot and headed in the direction of the fire, drawn to its strange beauty. As he approached the mountain, he heard a voice calling to him from the valley! Mūsa ﷺ cautiously followed the sound of the voice. As he came closer, he saw a tree blazing with brilliant and stunning flames, but for some strange reason, it was not being burnt. The voice that he had heard was coming from that tree!

The tree was a symbol of Allāh's power. Allāh ﷻ had decided that it was time for Mūsa ﷺ to become a prophet and guide his people to the true teachings of Islām.

Suddenly, Allāh ﷻ spoke to Mūsa ﷺ. "O Mūsa! Know that I am your Lord! Take off your shoes. You are in the Sacred Valley."[15]

Mūsa ﷺ could not believe what was happening. For a moment he was too shocked to move and he simply stared in wild-eyed amazement at what he was seeing and hearing. Once he had calmed down and realized that this was truly a Message from Allāh ﷻ, he quickly took off his shoes as a sign of respect.

Allāh ﷻ continued to speak to Mūsa ﷺ. "I have chosen you to be My Prophet. Listen carefully! I am Allāh; there is no god but Me. Therefore, serve Me and remember to pray to Me alone!"[16]

Allāh ﷻ then asked, "What is that in your right hand?"

Mūsa ﷺ humbly stuttered, "It.. it.. it is my staff. I lean on it; I use it to beat down leaves for my sheep to eat, and I use it for many other things."

"Throw it to the ground, O Mūsa," Allāh ﷻ commanded him.

Mūsa ﷺ immediately obeyed, throwing the staff to the ground. He was astonished to see the ordinary staff turn into a large snake that slithered at his feet. Mūsa's eyes were wide with amazement. Then Allāh ﷻ ordered him to pick up the snake. When Mūsa ﷺ did so, it turned back into a staff.[17] Allāh ﷻ then said to Mūsa ﷺ, "Put your hand close to your chest."[18]

Prophet Mūsa ﷺ again obeyed, and when he pulled his hand out, it was shining white with a radiant and divine light. Mūsa ﷺ stared in awe at his glowing hand. Allāh ﷻ showed Mūsa ﷺ these miracles as signs of His great power. These miracles made Mūsa ﷺ realize the Greatness of his Lord, and how blessed he was to be shown such favor.

"You are my Messenger. Go with these two Signs from your Lord to *Fir'awn* and his chiefs." Allāh ﷻ ordered. "They are wicked people who are doing much evil. Invite them to the Right Path."[19]

Prophet Mūsa ﷺ thought about his troubles in *Fir'awn*'s kingdom. His head began to swim with different thoughts. He was honored and excited to be appointed a Prophet like Shu'aib ﷺ, but at the same time he knew that it would not be an easy task. To make matters worse, Mūsa ﷺ had burned his tongue on a piece of coal when he was young, and that prevented him from speaking clearly.

He prayed to Allāh ﷻ for help. "O my Lord, open my heart so that I may learn more of Your Knowledge, and make it easy for me to bring Your Message to *Fir'awn*," he prayed. "Straighten my tongue so that I can speak clearly to the people."[20]

Prophet Mūsa ﷺ then added, "Oh my Lord, raise up someone from my family to help me. Hārūn, my brother, can add to my strength. Let him share my task."[21] Allāh ﷻ listened to Prophet Mūsa's prayer and then said, "Your prayers are answered. I will make you stronger with the help of your brother, Hārūn. Together, you will be so powerful that *Fir'awn* and his chiefs will not be able to hurt you. Go with My Signs. You, and all those who follow you, will be victorious. O Mūsa, I have chosen you, and you are ready to be my Servant."[22] Mūsa ﷺ took a deep breath and then returned quickly to his wife.

PROPHET MŪSA ﷺ AND PROPHET HĀRŪN ﷺ BRING ALLĀH'S MESSAGE

When Prophet Mūsa ﷺ returned to Egypt with Prophet Hārūn ﷺ, *Fir'awn* was shocked to see him. He remembered Mūsa ﷺ as a young man that had once lived in his palace. He was surprised to see that now Mūsa ﷺ had become a wise adult who was not afraid of him or his guards.

Prophet Mūsa ﷺ did not waste time when he met *Fir'awn*. "We have been sent to you by the Lord of all the Worlds," he said in a clear voice. "You have rebelled against Allāh. It is better for you to seek Allāh's Mercy. I will guide you to our Lord, Allāh, and show you the straight path." Then he said firmly, "Let Bani Isrā'il go with us and do not make them suffer anymore."[23B] *Fir'awn* laughed loudly at Prophet Mūsa's words. "Didn't we care for you when you were young?" he demanded. "Didn't we take you into our palace and let you live here for many years?[23] Why are you ungrateful to us? And who is this Lord of all the Worlds?"[24] he asked scornfully. It was obvious that *Fir'awn* did not like the idea of his people fearing something or someone other than himself.

Prophet Mūsa ﷺ stood bravely before *Fir'awn* and his men and answered, "I am speaking of the Lord of the Heavens and the Earth, and all that is in between."

Fir'awn looked around at the people in shock. "Did you hear what a silly thing he just said?" he asked in amusement.

Prophet Mūsa ﷺ remained calm, "The One I speak of is your Lord, and the Lord of all of your people."

Fir'awn became really angry. "The messenger that has sent you here is a crazy man," he said harshly, his eyes squinting in anger. "I am your god! If you take another god besides me, I will throw you in jail."[25]

Prophet Mūsa ﷺ was not frightened. He knew that Allāh ﷻ would protect him. He looked Fir'awn straight in the eye and asked, "What if I show you something that clearly proves that I am a Messenger from the Lord of all the Worlds?"

Just as Allāh ﷻ had told him to do, Prophet Mūsa ﷺ threw down his staff. To everyone's amazement, it turned into a slithering snake! The people could hardly believe their eyes. Those who were nearby stepped back in fear.

Then Prophet Mūsa ﷺ took his hand out from under his robe and raised it above his head. The people were dazzled by its shining brilliance. They had never seen anything like this before!

Fir'awn, however, was not impressed. He was certain that Mūsa ﷺ was performing some sort of magic trick. He did not understand that these were Signs from Allāh ﷻ to show the people that Prophets Mūsa ﷺ and Hārūn ﷺ were bringing a message of Truth.

"He is not a prophet. He is only a smart magician," *Fir'awn* said with a look of disgust on his face.

MŪSA ﷺ AGAINST THE MAGICIANS

When *Fir'awn*'s chiefs saw the miracles of Allāh ﷻ, they became afraid that the people might follow Prophet Mūsa ﷺ and Prophet Hārūn ﷺ and rise against *Fir'awn*. "Mūsa wants to take over your kingdom," the chiefs warned *Fir'awn*. "Something must be done."

"What should I do?" *Fir'awn* asked worriedly.

"Keep him and his brother here in the palace. Do not tell them our plan. We will send men all over the land to get the best magicians to challenge Mūsa."[26]

Their plan was to have a contest between Prophet Mūsa ﷺ and the best magician in all the kingdom. *Fir'awn*'s chiefs were sure that their magicians were much more powerful than Mūsa ﷺ. They decided to have the competition on the day of the big Temple Festival, an annual festival celebrated by all the people in

Egypt. *Fir'awn* wanted everyone in the kingdom to see Prophet Mūsa ﷺ defeated.

Word spread quickly throughout the land and magicians from all over the kingdom came to the palace to demonstrate their tricks. *Fir'awn* promised a great reward to any magician who could beat the Prophet.

The day of the festival finally arrived, and the townspeople gathered excitedly. The sun shone brightly on the colorfully decorated streets and temples of Egypt. Almost everyone from the town had come to watch the contest between Prophet Mūsa ﷺ and *Fir'awn*'s magicians. Everyone had an opinion as to who would win the contest, but no one ever imagined that they would witness something truly miraculous that day.

Prophet Mūsa ﷺ stood calmly in the center of the masses of people and faced the most skilled magicians in the land of Egypt. He had no fear because he knew that Allāh ﷻ would help him win the contest. It was agreed that the

Fir'awn's magicians would throw their sticks first.

One by one, the magicians threw their ropes and staffs on the ground. As the people watched, it appeared that the ropes and staffs had turned into tiny snakes that moved around the feet of the magicians. The snakes seemed almost real and not just a magic trick. The crowd began to roar in excitement, sensing that Mūsa ﷺ had met his match. A slight smile of victory formed on *Fir'awn*'s face.

Now it was Prophet Mūsa's turn. A hush fell over the crowd as everyone waited breathlessly to see what he would do. Mūsa ﷺ stepped forward, and just as Allāh ﷻ had taught him, he threw down his staff. To everyone's astonishment, Mūsa's staff transformed into a live snake, one that was much bigger than all the others. The snake quickly slithered towards the other ones and swallowed them up!

The crowd erupted in screams of disbelief and astonishment. The magicians shook their heads, because they knew that this was no magic trick. It was truly a miracle from Allāh ﷻ. Without hesitation, they fell down on their knees and bowed their heads down to the ground.

"We believe in Allāh ﷻ, the Lord of all the Worlds, the Lord of Mūsa and Hārūn,"[27] they exclaimed. When this happened, many of the onlookers gasped in shock.

Fir'awn became so angry at what he was seeing that he could barely speak. He rose from his throne and shook his fist at the magicians.

"How dare you believe in the Lord of Mūsa And Hārūn before *I* give you permission to!" he demanded. "I will cut off your hands and your feet and I will hang you on a cross where you will die!"[28] The magicians were not afraid of *Fir'awn*'s threats. "We believe in our Lord. Do you want to hurt us just because we believe in His Signs?" Then they turned to Allāh ﷻ. "Oh Allāh, have mercy on us," they prayed. "Forgive us for our wrongdoing. And when we die let us die as Muslims."[29]

Fir'awn's chiefs shook with fear. They were afraid that everyone would start following Prophet Mūsa ﷺ and not obey Fir'awn anymore. They quickly scanned the crowd, hoping that there would be no trouble for their embarrassed leader.

"How can you allow this to happen?" they asked Fir'awn. "They are going to make trouble in your kingdom. The people will stop believing in you and your gods."[30]

Deep down inside, Fir'awn was afraid of Prophet Mūsa ﷺ because he knew that Mūsa ﷺ really did bring a true Message from Allāh ﷻ. He knew that he could not convince Mūsa ﷺ that he was wrong, so he decided to threaten the people instead.

Pacing back and forth, he bellowed, "We will kill all the boys Bani Isrā'il! We will control them and dominate them!"[31] Prophet Mūsa ﷺ was not afraid of his threats. "Pray for help from Allāh ﷻ, and be patient and faithful. All things belong to Allāh ﷻ and He will help those who worship Him. If we keep faith in Allāh ﷻ, we will win."[32]

THE SEVEN SIGNS

Allāh ﷻ does not like arrogant people and He became very angry with *Fir'awn*. He decided to punish the *Fir'awn* and his people. He sent seven signs to show *Fir'awn* and his followers the Power He had over them.

The first of these signs was a widespread drought. For years, only a little rain fell on Egypt. The once fertile land became dry and dusty, preventing crops from growing properly. Because the crops had dried and withered away, there was not enough food to eat. The Egyptians became very frightened, and they finally pleaded with Prophet Mūsa ﷺ to ask Allāh ﷻ to stop the punishment. They were sorry for their past actions. They promised that if the drought ended, they would let the Children of Isrā'il go free and leave Egypt with him.

Prophet Mūsa ﷺ was very happy to hear this. He thought that the people finally believed in Allāh ﷻ and that they were sorry for their bad deeds. He thanked Allāh ﷻ for bringing the people to the Straight Path and he prayed for Allāh ﷻ to send rain.

Hearing Mūsa's prayer, Allāh ﷻ sent dark storm clouds that rolled across the sky and burst forth with sheets of pouring rain. The baked and cracked earth absorbed the pouring drops, and slowly became soft and fertile. The rain

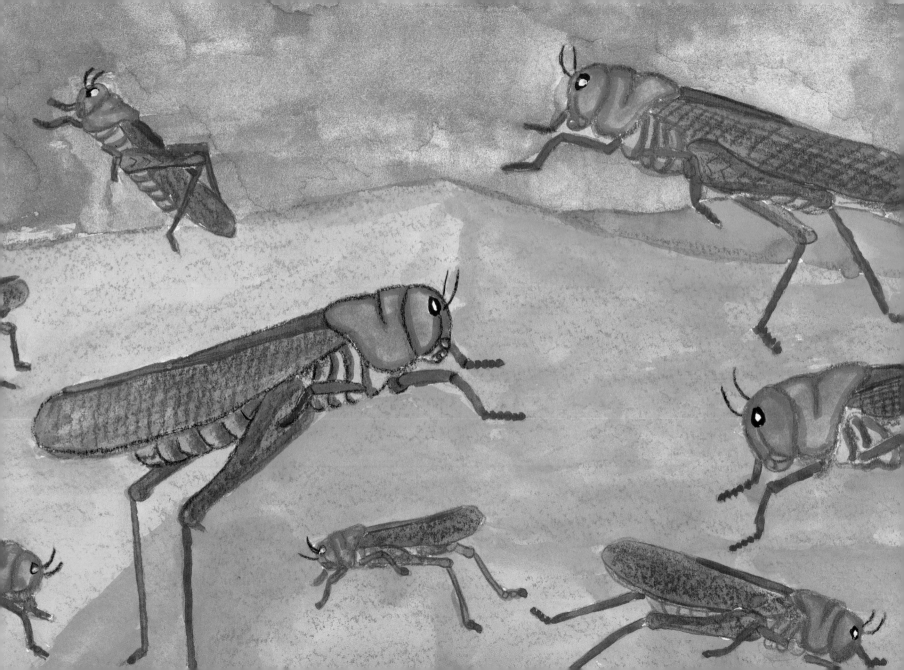

continued until the withered crops came back to life, growing lush and green. Once again, there was plenty of food for everyone. It seemed as if things were working for the best.

However, it was not long before the people broke their promise to Mūsa ﷺ. They did not thank Allāh ﷻ for the rain.

"*We* have brought the rain," they boasted. "We do not care what kind of Signs you bring," they told Mūsa ﷺ. "We will never believe in you."[33]

Even though they were ungrateful, Allāh ﷻ is Kind and Merciful, and He gave them many more chances to change their evil ways and ask Him for forgiveness. The next Great Sign was a contagious plague that killed hundreds of people. Then there came billions and billions of grasshoppers that ate all the crops and filled the air wherever the people turned. It was hard to even open one's mouth without grasshoppers entering it. Next, Allāh ﷻ sent a whole army of lice

to infest the animals. Then came hundreds of thousands of frogs. They seemed to be everywhere - in the food, in the water, and in the bedrooms. Finally, Allāh ﷻ turned the water in the Nile into a crimson river of blood.

Each time Allāh ﷻ sent a punishment *Fir'awn* and his people would promise Prophet Mūsa ﷺ that they would change their ways if the punishment ended. They would beg for Allāh's forgiveness and ask Mūsa ﷺ to give them another chance. But whenever Allāh ﷻ ended the punishment, they would forget their promise. Instead, they would go back to living and worshipping just as they had before.

Fir'awn felt powerless against Mūsa ﷺ and Allāh ﷻ. Knowing that people could see that he was losing control, *Fir'awn* decided to criticize Mūsa ﷺ.

He gathered all his people and said to them, "All of Egypt belongs to me. The Nile River flows under my palace. I am better than poor, pitiful Mūsa.

He cannot even speak clearly, like I can. And if he is so great, why does he not have any gold bracelets and chains? If he really is a Messenger, why didn't he bring angels with him?"[34]

At last, Prophet Mūsa ﷺ knew that there was no hope for *Fir'awn* and the people of Egypt. He went to the palace of *Fir'awn* and told him, "You have seen the Signs of Allāh ﷻ and you did not obey. There is no hope for you. I am certain that you will be one of those who will be destroyed."[35]

Mūsa ﷺ had not lost complete faith in all of the Egyptians, for Queen Āsiya ﷲ, the wife of *Fir'awn*, accepted Islām and became a leader of the believers. She decided to join Mūsa ﷺ and worship Allāh ﷻ, and this made the Prophet ﷺ extremely proud. Ever since he was young, he knew that she was a noble and respectable woman who always did righteous deeds. She was the one who had saved him long, long ago, when he was found floating on the River Nile in a basket. Now, decades later, Mūsa ﷺ was returning the favor by saving her soul.

Āsiya ﷺ prayed to Allāh ﷻ: "O my Lord! Build me a palace in *Jannah* and save me from *Fir'awn* and his disbelieving people."[36]

ESCAPE BY NIGHT

Even though the *Fir'awn* and his people had seen the seven great signs of Allāh ﷻ, they would not believe in Allāh ﷻ. They still would not set the Bani Isrā'il free.

Allāh ﷻ ordered Prophet Mūsa ﷺ to leave Egypt and to take all the people that believed in his message with him. Mūsa ﷺ secretly met with the Israelite people, telling them to pack their belongings and to be prepared for the night when they would escape. Word spread among the Bani Isrā'il, but none of them dared to spill their secret to *Fir'awn*. They waited anxiously for the night when Mūsa ﷺ would lead them away from the evil place they had been trapped in for generations.

One night, Mūsa ﷺ gave his people the news that they were to leave immediately. The Bani Isrā'il began to quietly gather their families and important belongings. They silently slipped out of their homes and away from the town under the cover of night. They went by horse, by cart, and by foot. There were people of all ages, from grandchildren to grandparents. Those who were stronger helped the weak carry their belongings. At last they were getting away from *Fir'awn* and his people.

With the help of Allāh ﷻ, Prophet Mūsa ﷺ and Prophet Hārūn ﷺ led thousands of followers out of Egypt, while the Egyptians slept. As the moon glowed above them in the still desert night, the Banī Isrā'il escaped further and further away from *Fir'awn*.

The next morning, *Fir'awn* received news that all of his slaves had left. He could hardly believe his ears. He flew into a rage. He quickly ordered his guards to go into the city to see what was happening. One by one, his guards came back to tell him that it was true. The homes of the Children of Isrā'il had indeed been deserted.

"The Banī Isrā'il are my slaves. They have made me very angry!"[37] *Fir'awn* growled. He held an emergency meeting with his advisors and they decided to gather an army to go after Prophet Mūsa ﷺ and the Banī Isrā'īl. *Fir'awn* swore that he would bring them back to Egypt and punish them severely. He would show them who was in charge.

Fir'awn spent the whole night organizing his army and making sure that his horses were prepared for the chase. As soon as the sun rose, *Fir'awn*'s forces set off after Prophet Mūsa ﷺ and the Children of Isrā'il.

THE RED SEA

By now, Prophet Mūsa ﷺ and his followers had travelled quite far. They had gone as far East as the Red Sea, which divided Egypt and Arabia. They were tired and exhausted from their sleepless night. The sea sparkled in front of them like a liquid jewel and they washed themselves in its cool and crystal waters.

They were talking excitedly to each other, knowing how close they were to a life of freedom when they heard something in the distance. One by one, they lowered their voices and stopped talking. They strained their ears to listen to the sound they heard in the distance. As the rumbling grew louder, they looked to the West. What they saw terrified them.

On the horizon was a large group of people on horseback, thousands of them, trailing a cloud of dust behind them. They were quickly making their way towards the Children of Isrā'il. As the horses drew closer, they could see that it was none other than *Fir'awn* and his army, coming to punish them.

Some of Prophet Mūsa's followers began to shake with fear. "It is the *Fir'awn* and his army!" they cried. "They are going to catch up with us!"[38] Prophet Mūsa ﷺ remained calm. He knew that Allāh ﷻ would help them. He told his people to be patient and not to be afraid. He ordered them to keep moving forward and trust in Allāh ﷻ to protect them. The Children of Isrā'il obeyed Prophet Mūsa ﷺ and slowly, they came closer to the edge of the Red Sea. They looked back and saw *Fir'awn*'s army coming closer and closer. The thundering of their horses' hooves grew louder and they could feel the ground shaking as the army approached. They looked around them. On one side was the army, on the other side was the wide open sea. They were trapped. Where would they go? They began to give up all hope.

"We are doomed!" they began to yell, knowing they had no weapons to fight with. "Mūsa, what are we going to do? What is the plan?" They clutched each other in fear, feeling that they were certainly doomed.

Actually, Prophet Mūsa ﷺ had no plan, but he was still calm, trusting that Allāh ﷻ would do something to protect them. When all of Prophet Mūsa's people had gathered at the edge of the sea, Allāh ﷻ ordered him to throw his staff into the water.

By now the army of *Fir'awn* was so close, that Mūsa's followers could clearly see their faces and hear them yelling. They turned in desperation to Mūsa ﷺ as he pulled out his staff. Then, he walked to the edge of the sea and

threw his staff in it. The people watched breathlessly to see what would happen.

To their astonishment, the Red Sea began to part into two, right before their very eyes! Each side of the sea rose up like a huge wall of water. In the middle of the two towering walls, a path was formed for Prophet Mūsa ﷺ and his people to cross to the other side. Thanking Allāh ﷻ for saving them, they hurried through the parted water as fast as they could. As they went, they looked above and around themselves in awe. Truly this was a miracle of Allāh ﷻ!

Meanwhile, *Fir'awn* and his army watched in shock. *Now they had seen everything*, they thought in amazement. Without another thought, *Fir'awn* followed Prophet Mūsa ﷺ and his people with his own army of soldiers. They were quickly gaining ground on the Bani Isrā'il and would catch them in a matter of minutes.

All people of Bani Isrā'il had already crossed the Red Sea and had safely reached the other side. They turned to look back and saw the army of thousands closing in on them. As *Fir'awn*'s army came thundering through the path, Allāh ﷻ ordered the sea to close. Instantly, the walls of water came crashing down. *Fir'awn* and his army could only look up and scream in terror as the sea violently crushed them.

As the waters of the Red Sea closed down upon *Fir'awn*, he cried out to Prophet Mūsa ﷺ to save him.

"I believe in your God," he screamed desperately. *"I believe in the God of the Banī Israī'il. Save me!"* He threw himself from his chariot and prostrated before Allāh ﷻ.

But it was too late. Allāh ﷻ had given *Fir'awn* many chances to earn His Mercy, but he had always refused to believe. As a sign of His great Power and Anger on those who would not believe in Him, Allāh ﷻ preserved *Fir'awn*'s body in the sea.[39]

THE GIFTS OF ALLĀH ﷻ TO THE BANĪ ISRĀ'IL

The Banī Isrā'il had been slaves to the kings of Egypt for four hundred years. At last, they were free. They travelled for many days and nights under the hot sun and cool desert nights. Allāh ﷻ had commanded Prophet Mūsa ﷺ to lead his people to the Promised Land, which would be the their new home, far away from the kings of Egypt.

After traveling a great distance, Prophet Mūsa ﷺ and his followers stopped at the Sinai Peninsula. They had been traveling for many months and his people were getting tired and angry. They wanted to rest. The Sinai Peninsula was mainly desert and they were homesick. They missed the shady green trees and cool blue waters of Egypt. They started to complain to Mūsa ﷺ about the hot sun and lack of food and water. Prophet Mūsa ﷺ loved his people and he did not

want them to be unhappy, so he prayed to Allāh ﷻ to help them.

Allāh ﷻ is Kind and Merciful, so He ordered the clouds to cover the sun. Large, cottony clouds rolled across the sun, completely covering it. Then He ordered flocks of quail to fly across the sky. Thousands and thousands of quail and droplets of sweet *Manna* fell upon the ground. The Banī Isrā'il were overjoyed.

There were some large rocks in the desert so Allāh ﷻ told Prophet Mūsa ﷺ "Strike the rock with your staff."[40] Another miracle happened! When Prophet Mūsa ﷺ struck the rock, twelve holes appeared in it. From each hole gushed a spring of clear, cold water. Each of the twelve tribes of the Banī Isrā'il now had its own spring. They had enough water for themselves as well as for their animals.

Allāh ﷻ gave the Banī Isrā'il many blessings. Whenever they asked for something, it was granted immediately. But they were still unsatisfied. "We do not like to eat the same kind of food every day," they complained to Mūsa ﷺ. "Pray to your Lord for some green herbs, cucumbers, beans, garlic and onions."[41]

Prophet Mūsa ﷺ finally became upset at his people for being so ungrateful. "What is the matter with you?" he asked them. "Do you want to have nice food to eat, or would you rather be safe from Fir'awn and his people? If you want those foods so much, just leave. Go and live in town where you can find all the nice things that you want."[42]

ALLĀH ﷻ GIVES PROPHET MŪSA ﷺ THE LAW

All people need laws so that they can live peacefully and happily together. When the Banī Isrā'il came to the Sinai Peninsula, they were no longer slaves. They no longer had to obey *Fir'awn*'s laws. Prophet Mūsa ﷺ needed new laws for his people.

Prophet Mūsa ﷺ was ordered by Allāh ﷻ to go to Mount Sinai. There, he would receive the Divine Laws for his people to follow and obey. When he was ready to go, he said to his brother, Prophet Hārūn ﷺ, "Take my place with my people and do what is right. Do not follow the path of the disbelievers."[43]

He took seventy men from the Children of Isrā'il, so that they could learn the Laws of Allāh ﷻ and go back to teach their people. These seventy men stayed at the foot of the mountain while Prophet Mūsa ﷺ went to the top of the mountain by himself.

When Prophet Mūsa ﷺ had reached the top, he called out to Allāh ﷻ: "O Allāh! Please let me see You so that I can look at You while we speak."[44] "You cannot see Me face to face," Allāh ﷻ replied. "Instead, look at that mountain over there."[45] Prophet Mūsa ﷺ looked over at the next mountain. He was awed to see that it instantly crumbled and fell to the ground in a heap of ashes and dust. Prophet Mūsa ﷺ bowed down on the ground, unable to speak.

"All Glory be to You," he said finally. "I ask for forgiveness. I am the first to believe in Your Power."[46] Allāh ﷻ then spoke. "O Mūsa! I have chosen you above all people. I have given you My Message and I have spoken directly to you. So obey the Laws that I give you and be thankful to Me for showing you the Straight Path."[47]

Then Prophet Mūsa ﷺ was given two stone tablets on which the Divine

Laws for his people were carved. The Laws taught people how to lead their daily lives in a pure and respectable manner. They taught them how to be good human beings and how to treat other people.

"Take these Laws back to your people," Allāh ﷻ commanded Prophet Mūsa ﷺ. "Teach them to your people and order them to follow them well."

PROPHET MŪSA ﷺ AND THE WISE MAN

Prophet Mūsa ﷺ was also given a special mission by Allāh ﷻ. He was told to find a certain wise man who would give him knowledge. Mūsa ﷺ was given a special fish to take on his journey. Allāh ﷻ did not tell Prophet Mūsa ﷺ where the wise man could be found. However, He told him that the man was at a place where two seas joined each other. Allāh ﷻ also told him that when he reached this place, he would forget about his fish and it would escape into the sea.

Mūsa ﷺ set off with his fish to look for the wise man who would give him the great knowledge that he desired. He took a servant with him for company. They journeyed for many months with no luck, but Prophet Mūsa ﷺ knew that he could not give up.

"I will not give up until I reach the junction of the two seas, even if I have to travel for many years," he said firmly.

Sometimes, they would stop to rest along the way. When they were ready to move on, they always remembered to take the special fish with them. They were very careful not to leave it behind. One day, however, when they stopped to rest, they laid the fish on a rock and Prophet Mūsa ﷺ fell asleep. His servant watched as the fish leaped from the rocks and disappeared into the sea.

Soon, the two set off again. After they had traveled for some time, Prophet Mūsa ﷺ asked his servant to bring them some breakfast. Suddenly, the servant remembered the fish. He told Mūsa ﷺ how the fish had escaped into the water at their last resting stop. "I forgot to tell you about it," he said to the Prophet.

Prophet Mūsa ﷺ became excited. "That is the place that we were looking for!" he exclaimed. "Let us go back there."

Prophet Mūsa ﷺ and his servant retraced their steps until they arrived at the place where the fish had jumped into the sea. There, they found the man they were looking for. His name was Al-Khidr.

"May I follow you and be your student, so that I may learn some of the Divine Wisdom that Allāh ﷻ has given you?" Mūsa ﷺ asked Al-Khidr.

"I do not think that you have enough patience to travel with me. You will not understand many of the things that I will do along the way," Al-Khidr replied.

"You will find that I am a very patient man and *Inshā' Allāh*, I will not cause you any trouble," Prophet Mūsa ﷺ quickly assured him.

"You may travel with me under one condition," proposed Al-Khidr. "The condition is that you may not ask me any questions about anything I do until I am ready to tell you why I did them."[48] Prophet Mūsa ﷺ agreed, and they began their journey together. They traveled for some time before they came upon some people with a boat. The boatmen offered the travelers a ride, and they agreed. Prophet Mūsa ﷺ followed Al-Khidr on to the boat and thanked the generous boatmen. When they had reached their destination and rose to exit the boat, Al-Khidr suddenly leaned down and put a hole in the bottom of the boat.

Prophet Mūsa ﷺ was shocked by this terrible act. After all, the boat did

not belong to him. The people who owned the boat were very poor, and they had been kind enough to give them a ride. "Do you want these kind people to drown?" he demanded Al-Khidr. "I cannot understand why you have done such a terrible thing."

Al-Khidr was not sorry for what he had done. "Didn't I tell you that you would not have enough patience to learn from me?" he asked Prophet Mūsa ﷺ.[49]

Prophet Mūsa ﷺ remembered his promise to Al-Khidr. "Forgive me and please do not be angry at me for losing my patience," he quickly apologized.[50]

Al-Khidr accepted his apology, and they continued on their way. Soon they came across a young boy who was playing. Mūsa ﷺ watched as Al-Khidr calmly walked over to the handsome child, and without any hesitation, grabbed the boy's head and snapped his neck, killing him. Prophet Mūsa ﷺ was so enraged and horrified that he could barely speak.

"How can you kill an innocent child?" he demanded, pointing an accusing finger at Al-Khidr. "This is an awful thing that you have done."

Again, Al-Khidr calmly replied, "Did I not tell you that you would not have enough patience with me?"[51] Prophet Mūsa ﷺ was immediately sorry, as he again remembered his promise to be patient. "If I ask one more question, do not let me travel with you anymore,"[52] he said. Prophet Mūsa ﷺ and Al-Khidr continued on their way. After traveling for a long while, they came to a town. They were hungry and tired from their long journey, so Al-Khidr asked the towns-people for some food and a place to rest. The people of the town refused to help them. They angrily told them to leave. As Prophet Mūsa ﷺ and Al-Khidr left, they passed by a wall that was so old, it was crumbling. Even though the towns-people had been unkind to them, Al-Khidr stopped to repair the wall.

Prophet Mūsa ﷺ watched with great interest as Al-Khidr worked.

"Maybe the people will pay you for fixing their wall," he remarked to Al-Khidr.[53]

"This is the end of our journey together," Al-Khidr said to Mūsa ﷺ as they left the town. Now I will tell you why I did all the things that I did along our way.

"The boat that I ruined belonged to some poor people. The king of that land is a greedy man. He was taking all the boats from the people and using them for his army. I put a hole in the boat so that the army would not want to take it."[54]

Allāh ﷻ had given Al-Khidr knowledge of all this. When the king's men came, they did not take the boat. The poor people easily repaired it and were able to keep it.

"As for the young boy," Al-Khidr continued, "he did not believe in Allāh ﷻ. His parents were righteous people. He was cruel to them because they were Muslims. Allāh ﷻ will give them another son who will be kind and obedient to them," Al-Khidr explained.[55]

"The wall that was falling down belonged to two orphaned children living in the town. Before their father died, he buried a treasure beneath the wall. Allāh ﷻ wanted the children to grow up before they found the treasure."[56] Prophet Mūsa ﷺ understood that if the wall had crumbled, the treasure would be found by the townspeople. They would not give it to the orphans.

"I did not do these things just because I felt like doing them," Al-Khidr informed Prophet Mūsa ﷺ.[57] "I was guided by Allāh ﷻ, Who knows and sees all things."

Prophet Mūsa ﷺ learned a lot from his teacher. He learned that things are not always what they appear to be. He also learned that Allāh ﷻ always does things for a very good reason, even though they may not make sense to us at the time. He realized that if he remained patient, he would understand why things happen the way that they do.

PROPHET MŪSA ﷺ AND HIS PEOPLE SEE THE PROMISED LAND

It was time for Prophet Mūsa ﷺ to return to his people. He had been gone for a very long time. The Banī Isrā'īl were still living in the Sinai Peninsula where he had left them.

When Prophet Mūsa ﷺ returned to his people, he told them that they were going to set out to find the Promised Land. He sent twelve men, one from each tribe, to find the homeland that Allāh ﷻ had promised them.

The twelve men travelled for some time before they found the Land. They could hardly believe their eyes. It was a rich and beautiful place. There were green hills and valleys as far as they could see. Lush orchards grew

delicious fruit in abundance. There was pomegranate, fig and plump grapes. It was even more beautiful than the scenery of Egypt, the land they missed so dearly. The twelve men took as many as fruits as they could carry to show their people.

They would return to this beautiful land with all their family and friends and live here forever. Their children would be born here and never again would they be slaves to anyone. At last, they had a home to call their own.

However, there was one problem. In this beautiful land, there lived people who did not like outsiders. They were strong and tough, and this scared Prophet Mūsa's people. They knew that these people would fight until death to keep the Banī Isrā'īl out of the land.

The twelve men returned to tell their people the news. "We will not be able to fight such strong men," they told the people. "They will certainly destroy us."

The Banī Isrā'il became frightened when they heard the news. They did not want to fight men who were bigger or more powerful than them.

Prophet Mūsa ﷺ was angry at his people for being such cowards. He wanted them to work for what was rightfully theirs. He wanted them to fight for what they believed in. He knew that Allāh ﷻ would help them win the Promised Land.

"O my people!" he told them. "Go to the Holy Land which Allāh ﷻ has promised you. Do not stop trusting in Him. If you do so, you will lose everything."[58]

The Banī Isrā'il were not satisfied. "Oh, Mūsa," they said. "The people in that land are very strong. We will never go there until they leave."[59]

Joshua and Caleb were two of the men who had gone to see the Holy Land. They were true believers in Allāh ﷻ and His messenger. They were not afraid to fight these big men.

"We can fight them at the gate of the city," they told their people.

"Once we are inside the city, we can take over. Put your trust in Allāh ﷻ if you believe in Him."[60] The people were still not convinced. "You go with your Lord and fight them," they told Mūsa ﷺ and the few people who believed in him. "We will stay here until you come back."

Prophet Mūsa ﷺ was very sad to see that his people had such little faith and courage. Allāh ﷻ had saved them and blessed them time and time again, yet they still refused to put their faith in Him. Did they think that they had escaped Egypt and *Fir'awn*'s army simply because of luck?

Again, he turned to his followers and pleaded, "Why do you have no courage? Didn't you escape slavery in Egypt and the army of *Fir'awn* by putting your faith in Allah ﷻ? This situation is no different!"

But still his followers refused to join him. It was clear to Mūsa ﷺ that no matter what he said or did, they were not going to agree to enter the Promised Land unless people living there had left.

Mūsa ﷺ knew that there was nothing else he could do. He turned to Allāh ﷻ and prayed: "O my Lord! I have no power over anyone but myself and my brother. Remove us from these disobedient people."[61] Once again, Allāh ﷻ was not happy at the Children of Isrā'il. Allāh ﷻ told Prophet Mūsa ﷺ that He would punish them like He had punished the Egyptians for refusing to obey Him.

The punishment from Allāh ﷻ was that He would not allow the Children of Isrā'il to enter the Promised Land for forty years. During this time, they would be stuck in the desert. And so, it happened.

For forty years, the Children of Israel wandered aimlessly throughout the harsh Arabian desert. No blessings were bestowed upon them. There was no *Manna* and no *Salwa*, no crystal springs of water to quench their thirst, and no clouds to shield them from the glaring sun. For four decades, the sun beat down on them and the sand whipped mercilessly around them.

One of the greatest tragedies was that both Prophet Mūsa ﷺ and Hārūn ﷺ passed away during this time. The two people who had cared for the Banī Isrā'il the most, and who had rescued them from decades of slavery, died in the horrible conditions created by the Banī Isrā'il's refusal to obey Allāh ﷻ. The people had not only lost their Promised Land, they had also lost their Prophets. But even this was not enough to make them want to capture the Promised Land.

THE NEXT GENERATION OF THE CHILDREN OF ISRĀ'IL

By the time the forty years had passed, even those Bani Isrā'il who had disobeyed Allāh ﷻ and His prophets had also died. The generation that had gown up in slavery and cowardice was gone, leaving behind a new generation, which had grown in the harsh climate and environment of the desert. This new generation was young and brave. They did not want to spend the rest of their lives in misery like their parents. They wanted to live in the blessed Promised Land, and they would do whatever it took to make it their home.

Joshua became the leader of the Children of Isrā'il, and he was finally able to organize them into a willing and courageous army. With great faith and little fear, he led them across the River of Jordan and into the Holy Land called Palestine. With determination and the help of Allāh ﷻ they defeated the non-believing and greedy people there, and claimed it as their own home.

After centuries of slavery and decades of wandering, the Bani Isrā'īl were finally home.

Prophet Hārūn عليه السلام

HĀRŪN ﷺ IS CALLED TO BE ALLĀH'S MESSENGER

Hārūn ﷺ was a kind and gentle young man who lived in the country of Egypt. He was the elder brother of Prophet Mūsa ﷺ and came from the tribe of Banī Isrā'il (the Children of Isrā'il). At the time of his birth, his people were suffering greatly at the hands of the Egyptians, who had enslaved them for hundreds of years. The Fir'awn and his chiefs did everything in their power to keep the Israelites under their command.

As Hārūn ﷺ and Mūsa ﷺ grew older, they also grew in wisdom and in righteousness. They were known to be two of the most respectful and polite men in the land. Allāh ﷻ planned to make Mūsa ﷺ a prophet, because his peaceful and caring nature would help lead the people towards the Truth.

"Take My Clear Signs and go to Fir'awn and his chiefs, for he is doing a great deal of evil in this land," commanded Allāh ﷻ to His new prophet.

"O Allāh, please give me a helper from my family," prayed Prophet Mūsa ﷺ. "Send my brother Hārūn ﷺ with me so that I will be stronger. And make him share my duty with me, so that together, we may praise You all the time and never forget You."[1]

Mūsa ﷺ knew that his task would not be easy, and that if he had the help of his brother, he would have a greater chance of success. Mūsa ﷺ was also worried about his speech. When he was a child he had burned his tongue, so he did not speak clearly.

"My brother Hārūn ﷺ is a much better speaker than I am," explained Mūsa ﷺ. "Send him with me so that we both can show them the True Signs. I fear that they will not believe me if I go alone."[2]

"You have been given all that you asked for," assured Allāh ﷻ. "Do not be afraid because I am with you. I see and hear all things. So go, both of you, to Fir'awn and say: Behold! We are messengers sent by your Lord. Let the Children of Isrā'il go with us and do not cause them any more pain and suffering."[3]

PROPHET HĀRŪN ﷺ HELPS MŪSA ﷺ

Prophets Hārūn ﷺ and Mūsa ﷺ approached Fir'awn and his chiefs in the Royal Palace. "We have been sent by the Lord and Cherisher of all the Worlds," they announced. "Let the Children of Isrā'il go with us and do not cause them any more harm."[4]

Fir'awn and his chiefs laughed heartily. There was no way that they would set their slaves free. Who would do all the work if they were freed? They refused to obey.

As Allāh ﷻ had promised, He sent seven clear signs of His Power upon the Fir'awn and his people, yet they continued to enslave the Bani Isrā'il and worship their idols. Mūsa ﷺ and Hārūn ﷺ were finally ordered by Allāh ﷻ to take the believers and escape by night. They planned their escape carefully. One night, while the city slept, they crept away into the desert. Though Fir'awn and his mighty army followed them to capture and kill them, Allāh ﷻ saved the Banī Isrā'il. He crushed the King and his army and drowned them as they were crossing the Red Sea on the same Path that He had made for the believers. The believers thanked Allāh ﷻ for this miracle and continued on their way.

PROPHET HĀRŪN ﷺ TAKES RESPONSIBILITY

The Children of Isrā'il were finally freed after centuries of being slaves to the Fir'awn. The worst was behind them and the future held great

promise and opportunity.

They stopped to rest at the Sinai Peninsula and set up camp there. Once they settled in, Prophet Mūsa ﷺ was ordered by Allāh ﷻ to climb Mount Sinai to receive the Divine Laws. The Divine Laws would provide guidance for the believers and teach them right from wrong. Mūsa ﷺ informed the Banī Isrā'īl that he would be gone for forty days and forty nights. He appointed his brother Hārūn ﷺ to take his place as their leader.

"Take my place with my people and do what is right," he told Hārūn ﷺ.[5] "Do not follow the path of those who do wrong." Then he turned to his followers and told them to obey Hārūn ﷺ because he was also a Prophet of Allāh ﷻ. Then, Mūsa ﷺ said goodbye to his people and headed towards the mountain.

While Mūsa ﷺ was gone, Hārūn ﷺ dealt with the Bani Isrā'il in a respectful and caring manner, as he had always done. However, a great number of the people were not patient and were unwilling to remain obedient during Mūsa's absence. Many of these people had weak faith and they were not true believers.

Among these weak people was a man called the Sāmirī. It was not long after Mūsa's departure that he became restless and sinister. He could sense that many of the others were unhappy waiting for Mūsa ﷺ to take them to the Promised Land. He overheard people saying that they were upset with the situation and he himself began starting such discussions. Gradually, the people began to insist that if Allāh ﷻ truly existed, they should be able to see Him. They felt that if other people had idols, they should also have something similar which they could see and touch. Apparently, the miracles that Allāh ﷻ had provided for them by setting them free and helping them across the Red Sea were not enough to give them full faith.

The Sāmirī had an idea. He decided to create a god for them to worship.

He excitedly made his way around the various people, collecting jewelry and gold from everyone. He told them that he was doing it for the sake of Allāh ﷻ. The people began digging into their belongings and throwing their valuables to him. Then, he started a large bonfire and threw the gold into the searing flames.

The people gathered and began to cheer excitedly. When all the gold had melted, Sāmirī withdrew the bubbling liquid and formed it into the shape of a calf. People began throwing the jewelry from around their necks into the fire, howling with delight. The Sāmirī covered the crudely shaped calf in glittering necklaces and bracelets.

"This golden calf is your god and the god of Mūsa!" he yelled to the frenzied masses. "But Mūsa has forgotten."[6]

He held the shimmering calf high enough for all to see and the crowd erupted into cheers. The calf seemed to make a lowing sound, as real calves do,

and this made the people even more obsessed with the idol. They rushed to touch and kiss it. They bowed before it in adoration.

When Hārūn ﷺ came out and saw what was happening, he could not believe his eyes. He looked around in disbelief. He was shocked that the people could forget all that they had been taught in such a short period of time. His disappointment soon turned to anger, and he rushed towards the crowd in a rage.

"O my people!" he yelled to get their attention. "Stop this nonsense! This is a test of your faith. Resist the temptation, for Allāh ﷻ is Most Gracious. Follow me and obey my command!" he pleaded with them.[7]

"No!" they yelled back in unison. "We refuse to abandon this practice and we shall continue to do it until Mūsa returns to us!"[8] Hārūn ﷺ could see the mad passion in their eyes. They were clearly lost people. Still, he could not give up and let them commit this grave and serious sin.

Hārūn ﷺ decided to change his tactics. He attempted to reason with them and show them the error of what they were doing, but they refused to listen to his lectures. They screamed at him and threatened to hurt him if he continued to bother them. But Hārūn ﷺ knew that his duty was to help them see the Truth, so he continued to plead with them. Finally, the crazed people were so angered by him that they turned on him.

They chased him and grabbed him. Then they held him down, beating him with their fists and kicking him repeatedly, landing blow after blow upon the poor prophet's body and head. As they beat him, they growled, "If you continue with your protests, we will kill you!"

Prophet Hārūn ﷺ dragged himself away from them, realizing that it was no use trying to help them. With a heavy and bruised heart, he wept and prayed to Allāh ﷻ to forgive them and help them to see the Truth. He prayed that Mūsa ﷺ

would return soon to help.

MŪSA ﷺ RETURNS TO HIS FOLLOWERS

Mūsa ﷺ was informed by Allāh ﷻ that the Sāmirī had led the people astray. Following his Creator's orders, the Prophet rushed down the mountainside as quickly as he could. He knew that every minute counted. When he arrived at the campsite and saw the condition of his people, he became infuriated. Allāh ﷻ had done so much for them and this was how they showed their thanks. He rushed to his brother and grabbed him, angrily demanding an explanation. "O Hārun, what kept you from stopping them when they began to go astray?"[9]

Hārun ﷺ replied apologetically, "O son of my mother, please do not grab me by the beard or by the hair on my head. I was afraid you would think that I had caused this division among the Children of Isrā'il and that I had not respected your orders." He hastily explained what had happened and how he had nearly been killed in an attempt to stop them.

"The people would not listen to me and they even came close to killing me," explained Hārūn ﷺ to his brother. "Do not make them happy by being angry with me, and do not consider me to be one of those who has sinned."[10]

Saddened by this turn of events, Mūsa ﷺ prayed to Allāh ﷻ very passionately, asking for Him to forgive both of them for having let their followers go astray. Mūsa ﷺ then turned to the Sāmirī to get to the bottom of the incident.

"What do you have to say for yourself, Sāmirī?" demanded Mūsa ﷺ .[11]

He replied, "I took a handful of dust from the footprint of the Messenger and threw it into the calf. This is simply what I felt like doing, so I did it."[12]

Sāmirī showed no traces of guilt or embarrassment over what he had done.

"Get out of here and do not associate yourself with us," Mūsa ﷺ ordered in disgust. "Your punishment is that you will be cast away from us and isolated from civilization. Now watch as we melt your god in this fire and throw it into the sea."

The Sāmirī and the Banī Isrā'il watched in silent shame as the calf was melted in the fire. As it turned to liquid and began to lose shape, it became clear to them that the calf was not a god at all, but merely an idol. When it had dissolved into charred ashes, the Prophets ﷺ took the remains and tossed them into the sea. Everyone watched silently as the water hissed and sizzled from contact with the ashes. Much like the calf, their faith had vanished in a thin plume of smoke.

THE CHILDREN OF ISRĀ'ĪL REFUSE TO ENTER THE HOLY LAND

Even though the Children of Isrā'il had allowed themselves to be led astray and influenced by the Sāmirī, Allāh ﷻ showed His infinite Mercy by forgiving them and providing them with yet another chance to earn His Favor. Allāh ﷻ provided them with many blessings, giving them every reason to devote their lives to Him and His Prophets. But the Children of Isrā'il were clearly not mature enough to understand that. They continued to complain about the new land they had settled in, saying that it was not as pretty as Egypt. They complained about the food that Allāh ﷻ sent from Heaven. They were like disobedient children who were never satisfied.

Therefore, it came as no surprise when they refused to enter the beautiful Promised Land, to which twelve of their chiefs had been led by Allāh ﷻ.

Even though that land had everything they could possibly desire, they refused to go there because they feared the strong people who already lived there.

In a hateful way, they said, "We will never enter that land until the strong people that live there leave. They will destroy us. Mūsa and Hārūn, you go and fight them. We will wait here."[13]

Prophet Mūsa ﷺ and Hārūn ﷺ, joined by a few of the righteous believers, tried to convince the Banī Isrā'il that Allāh ﷻ would help them just like He always did, but they still refused to change their minds. They made it very clear that they would not enter the Promised Land until it was completely safe. They had lived in slavery for generations, and now that they were free, they wanted everything to be done for them. Allāh ﷻ became so angry with them that He decided to punish them.

He ordered Mūsa ﷺ and Hārūn ﷺ to keep their people in the harsh and rough wilderness for a period of forty years. They would not be allowed to enter the Promised Land until then. For forty years, the Bani Isrā'il wandered aimlessly in the searing desert heat that hung over the dry and dusty land. Allāh ﷻ and His Prophets had given them every opportunity to change their ways but it was hopeless.

When forty years had passed, many of the people had died and a new generation had taken their place. This new generation were true believers and they wanted to serve Allāh ﷻ alone. They did not want to live the rest of their lives in the desert as their parents had before them, so they obeyed Allāh's Command and set out to find the Promised Land. In time, they bravely entered the land and settled there comfortably.

Prophet Yūsuf ﷺ

1	Yūsuf 12:4
2	Yūsuf 12:5-6
3	Yūsuf 12:9
4	Yūsuf 12:9-10
5	Yūsuf 12:11-12
6	Yūsuf 12:13
7	Yūsuf 12:14
8	Yūsuf 12:16
9	Yūsuf 12:18
10	Yūsuf 12:19
11	Yūsuf 12:20
12	Yūsuf 12:21
13	Yūsuf 12:23-25
14	Yūsuf 12:36-37
15	Yūsuf 12: 41
16	Yūsuf 12: 42
17	Yūsuf 12: 43
18	Yūsuf 12: 45
19	Yūsuf 12:47-49
20	Yūsuf 12:50-51
21	Yūsuf 12:55
22	Yūsuf 12:58
23	Yūsuf 12:59
24	Yūsuf 12:61
25	Yūsuf 12:62
26	Yūsuf 12:63
27	Yūsuf 12:64
28	Yūsuf 12:65
29	Yūsuf 12:66

30	Yūsuf 12:67	45	Yūsuf 12:92-93
31	Yūsuf 12:69	46	Yūsuf 12:94
32	Yūsuf 12:70	47	Yūsuf 12:95
33	Yūsuf 12:71	48	Yūsuf 12:96
34	Yūsuf 12:72	49	Yūsuf 12:97
35	Yūsuf 12:73	50	Yūsuf 12:100
36	Yūsuf 12:78	51	Yūsuf 12:101
37	Yūsuf 12:79		
38	Yūsuf 12:80-81		

Prophet Shu'aib ﷺ

39	Yūsuf 12:83
40	Yūsuf 12:85
41	Yūsuf 12:86-87
42	Yūsuf 12:88
43	Yūsuf 12:89
44	Yūsuf 12:89-90

1	Al-A'rāf 7:85-86
2	Hūd 11:87
3	Hūd 11:88-89
4	Hūd 11:91
5	Al-A'rāf 7:90
6	Al- A'rāf 7:87

7	Al-A'rāf 7:88	12	Al-Qaṣaṣ 28:26
8	Al-A'rāf 7:93	13	Al-Qaṣaṣ 28:27
		14	Al-Qaṣaṣ 28:29

Prophet Mūsa ﷺ

1	ṬāHa 20 39	15	ṬāHā 20:12
2	Al-Qaṣaṣ 28:9	16	ṬāHā 20:13-14
3	Al-Qaṣaṣ 28:12	17	ṬāHā 20:17-20
4	Al-Qaṣaṣ 28:15	18	ṬaHa 20: 22
5	Al-Qaṣaṣ 28:16	19	Al-Qaṣaṣ 28:32
6	Al-Qaṣaṣ 28:19	20	ṬāHā 20:25-28
7	Al-Qaṣaṣ 28:20	21	Sūrah ṬāHā 20: 29-32
8	Al-Qaṣaṣ 28:21	22	ṬāHā 20:41-43
9	Al-Qaṣaṣ 28:23	23	Ash-Shu'arā' 26:16-18
10	Al-Qaṣaṣ 28:25	24	Ash-Shu'arā' 26:23
11	Al-Qaṣaṣ 28:25	25	Ash-Shu'arā' 26:24-29
		26	Ash-Shu'arā' 26: 34-37

27	Al-A'rāf 7:121-122		42	Al-Baqarah 2:61
28	Al-A'rāf 7:123-124		43	Al-A'rāf 7:142
29	Al-A'rāf 7:125-126		44	Al-A'rāf 7:143
30	Al-A'rāf 7:127		45	Al-A'rāf 7:143
31	Al-A'rāf 7:127		46	Al-A'rāf 7:143
32	Al-A'rāf 7:128		47	Al-A'rāf 7:144
33	Al-A'rāf 7:132		48	Al-Kahf 18:66-70
34	Az-Zukhruf 43: 51-53		49	Al-Kahf 18:71-72
35	Al-Muminūn 23:48		50	Al-Kahf 18:72-73
36	At-Taḥrīm 66:11		51	Al-Kahf 18:74-75
37	Ash-Shu'arā' 26: 54-56		52	Al-Kahf 18:76
38	Ash-Shu'arā' 26:61		53	Al-Kahf 18:77
39	Yūnus 10: 90		54	Al-Kahf 18:79
40	Al-Baqarah 2:60		55	Al-Kahf 18:80-81
41	Al-Baqarah 2:61		56	Al-Kahf 18:82

57	Al-Kahf 18:82		9	ṬāHā 20:93
58	Māi'dah 5:21		10	Al A'rāf 7:150
59	Al-Mā'idah 5:22		11	ṬāHā 20:95
60	Al-Mā'idah 5:23		12	ṬāHā 20:96
61	Al-Mā'idah 5:25		13	Al-Mā'idah 5:24

Prophet Hārūn ﷺ

1   ṬāHā 20:29-34

2   Al-Qaṣaṣ 28:34

3   ṬāHā 20: 46-47

4   Ash-Shu'arā' 26: 16-17

5   Al-A'rāf 7:142

6   ṬāHā 20:88

7   ṬāHā 20:90

8   ṬāHā 20:91

About the Author
Suhaib Hamid Ghazi

Suhaib Ghazi was born in Boston, Massachusettes in 1972. He has lived in California, Minnesota, Illinois, and Saudi Arabia. The author earned his undergraduate degree from the University of Redlands (CA) with a double major in Business Administration and Political Science. He is currently attending Law School at the University of Illinois at Champaign.